UNHOOKED

HOW TO QUIT ANYTHING

DR. FREDERICK WOOLVERTON
and SUSAN SHAPIRO

SKYHORSE PUBLISHING

Skyhorse Publishing books may be purchased in bulk at special discounts
for sales promotion, corporate gifts, fund-raising, or educational purposes.
Special editions can also be created to specifications. For details, contact the
Special Sales Department, Skyhorse Publishing, 307 West 36th Street,
11th Floor, New York, NY 10018 or info@skyhorsepublishing.com.

Skyhorse® and Skyhorse Publishing® are registered trademarks of
Skyhorse Publishing, Inc.®, a Delaware corporation.

Visit our website at www.skyhorsepublishing.com

10 9 8 7 6 5 4 3 2 1

Library of Congress Cataloging-in-Publication Data is available on file.

ISBN: 978-1-61608-418-9

Printed in the United States of America

ADVANCE PRAISE FOR *UNHOOKED*

"Addiction is one of the most fearsome challenges to happiness. *Unhooked* is crammed with insights and practical strategies to help you conquer addiction—whether you're addicted to drugs, alcohol, cigarettes, shopping, video games, exercising, or diet soda—and to help you gain your freedom and a happier life." —Gretchen Rubin, author of *The Happiness Project*, #1 *New York Times* bestseller.

"*Unhooked* offers new, powerful yet simple strategies to help you break free from the stranglehold of drugs, alcohol, food, gambling, smoking and other self-sabotage. Dr. Woolverton's personal odyssey and compelling client stories make it a great read. More importantly, his insights make the book an invaluable tool to regain control of your life."—Diana Kirschner, PhD, psychologist, author of bestseller *Love in 90 Days* and *Sealing the Deal*.

"One of life's great paradoxes is that the barriers to improvement are internal. Why do we have so much trouble making good choices? In *Unhooked*, a user's manual to improve your life, Frederick Woolverton draws upon his decades of experience helping people to teach us how to change for the better. An insightful, practical, and fun guide to self-improvement and happiness."—Terry Burnham, PhD, Harvard economics professor and coauthor of *Mean Genes: From Sex to Money to Food: Taming Our Primal Instincts*.

"What most impresses me about Fred Woolverton's addiction theories is his unapologetic demand that the patients face, experience, and tolerate their own suffering. It's a very spiritual position. You don't get that insight just by being a reformed addict. In addition to being a smart, well-trained, gifted therapist, Woolverton has the wisdom that can only be gained by deep early suffering. Luckily, he shares that hard-won wisdom with his patients and readers."—John D. Gartner, PhD, assistant professor of psychiatry at Johns Hopkins and author of *The Hypomanic Edge* and *In Search of Bill Clinton: A Psychological Biography*.

"A highly personal and compelling read. *Unhooked* takes the most complex subject in mental health—addictions—and puts forth a new treatment paradigm without applying a one-size-fits-all approach."—Vatsal Thakkar, MD, director of the graduate medical education wellness team at NYU Medical Center, and author of the textbooks *Addiction* and *Depression and Bipolar Disorder.*

"In a wise, engaging, first-person voice filled with empathy and humor, *Unhooked* offers brilliant, insightful, and inventive tactics on how to conquer the bad habits keeping you from getting what you want." —Karen Salmansohn, bestselling author of *How to Be Happy Dammit* and *The Bounce Back Book: How to Thrive In the Face of Adversity, Setbacks and Losses.*

"*Unhooked*'s intelligent, incisive plan will provide a straight shot (as long as it's not whiskey) to success."—Wendy Shanker, author of *The Fat Girl's Guide to Life* and *Are You My Guru?*

"Millions of Americans who are hooked on sugar, caffeine, diet foods, texting, emailing, painkillers, pornography, overeating, bulimia, and other unhealthy habits need *Unhooked*. This empowering book from veteran addiction specialist Dr. Frederick Woolverton compassionately guides addicts on a journey of self-discovery so that they can finally overcome the counterproductive behaviors that distract and prevent them from getting what they really want."—Connie Bennett, author of *Sugar Shock: How Sweets and Simple Carbs Can Derail Your Life.*

"*Unhooked* makes the solution to the grave problem of addiction very accessible, taking the embarrassment out of it. It's fascinating when an effective therapist explains his approach. The book makes you want to see Dr. Woolverton. His spirit and optimism perfuse every page." —Dr. Mary Pressman, child psychiatrist and assistant clinical professor at Mount Sinai Medical Center.

"*Unhooked* is great. The world really needs this book!"—Sherene Schostak, MA, Jungian psychoanalyst and author of *Surviving Saturn's Return: Overcoming the Most Tumultuous Time of Your Life.*

TO BOB COOK,

with gratitude

AUTHOR'S NOTE

Many former and current patients and colleagues generously granted me permission to use their stories in this book for the purpose of helping others overcome similar addictions. I have changed names, dates, and identifying characteristics for literary cohesion and to protect their privacy.

CONTENTS

INTRODUCTION

Dr. Frederick Woolverton's Personal and Professional Connection

Treating addicts has never been just about work, scientific data, or abstract theories for me. I am particularly sensitive to both the literal and the hidden repercussions of addiction because as a child I was severely traumatized by an alcoholic parent.

Growing up, my siblings and I used to spend holidays at my grandparents' house in Glen Cove, Long Island. I recall a lot of drinking, smoking, and laughing. Although it was the fifties, it seemed *Great Gatsby*-like. One Christmas when I was ten years old, my two brothers and I were included in the big family soiree. My mother, Mary, a dark-haired actress who looked beautiful that night in a satin blue dress and pearls, drank several mint juleps in a row, as she often did. Made of bourbon, sugar, and ice and garnished with sprigs of mint, mint juleps were her favorite drink. Early in the evening she seemed relaxed and happy, her face glowing as she told me, "You look so nice tonight, Freddy. Do you want to open some of your presents early?" This was an uncharacteristically warm offer from a mother who was usually strict, severe, and cold.

As the evening wore on, she followed her cocktails with glasses of red wine. I noticed her face was getting more red and flushed as it always did when she kept drinking. Afterwards I was eager to help her clean up, bringing leftover food and glasses back into the kitchen. As I handed her a dish, she spun around and out of the blue snapped, "You are nothing! You are no good! You are just like your father. You will never amount to anything!" The sudden change in her demeanor shocked me.

Although my mother had been drinking ever since I could remember, this was the first time I became aware of how alcohol could change someone's personality so dramatically. From warm and attentive, she became disturbed and enraged beyond reason. At that moment, I was amazed by the power that liquor could have. My mother continued to drink and to be physically and emotionally abusive throughout the rest of my childhood and teenage years. When I was fourteen, I wasn't surprised when I found out that my parents were getting divorced.

As a nineteen-year-old college sophomore, I was asked to testify at a custody trial for my ten-year-old sister, my youngest sibling. I did not yet realize this would make me part of the ongoing warfare that had taken over my parents' lives and that their children had become pawns in their battle. In order to protect my sister, I told the truth about my mother's alcoholism. Our family's unspoken rule was that nobody was ever allowed to mention it, especially in public. Enraged that I had humiliated her, my mother told me that day that she would never talk to me again. Her decision was swift and final. She cut off all contact and we didn't speak for more than thirty years. During that time I heard from relatives that she continued to drink into her eighties. I was a first-hand witness to the havoc and trauma that an addiction can wreak on an entire family.

Although genetic links underlying addictions have been well documented, alcohol never appealed to me much. After one night of doing tequila shots with college classmates, when I became so drunk I wound up violently sick, I lost any desire to ever get drunk again. Since then I've only had the occasional glass of wine. Cigarettes, however, held a strong allure. I first tried them when I was twelve years old and by fifteen I was smoking regularly. I loved everything about the habit and remained a-pack-a-day nicotine addict for twenty-three years. Even after the physical dangers of smoking were publicized, I put it in a different category than hard liquor or illegal drugs. Surely cigarettes were less dangerous than getting high on marijuana or cocaine, right? Nobody killed anybody driving while under the influence of Marlboros, I rationalized. This was before studies came out about the dangers of second-hand smoke.

In the 1980s, while working at the Baldwin Council Against Drug Abuse in Long Island, a community clinic that specialized in treating addictions, I told an alcoholic patient he was relying on vodka to soothe himself so he could better function with his wife, family, and in social situations. As I spoke, it occurred to me that I was describing myself. At that point I saw that his dependency on a bottle of vodka in his liquor cabinet was in many ways the same as my reliance on the reassuring presence of the pack of cigarettes in my shirt pocket.

I attempted to quit. I tried not smoking until 5:00 PM, but wound up going through my whole daily pack in fewer hours. Next I cut back to half a pack a day, but then I felt agitated and ran out at late hours to get more. I bought plastic cigarettes, chewed on straws, and sipped seltzer every time I wanted a cigarette, but none of these were satisfying or successful. I had no idea how difficult it would be to give up this crutch. Like many addicts, I kept trying to stop, failing, and then, in frustration, returned full steam to my habit. Although I had always seen myself as a sober and solid citizen, it was hard to admit that I was a substance abuser. I was an addiction specialist who was an addict myself.

One day I caught sight of myself reaching for a pack of cigarettes and it struck me: I had been using nicotine as self-medication to take the edge off my nervousness and anxiety, to maintain a level of calm throughout my workday, and to feel more socially confident. There was something reassuring about carrying a pack and a lighter that I reached for in times of stress. Just having my unfiltered Camels in my pocket, even without sparking one up, calmed me in a way nothing else could. Breathing in smoke felt satisfying and filling. I told my patients that "addicts depend on substances, not people," but somehow hadn't seen how perfectly that described me.

At the time, I was in a marriage that lacked emotional closeness and intimacy—with a wife who also smoked. In retrospect, I was strikingly closed off, selfish, and stuck in a lonely cycle of smoking hourly for self-soothing, with nobody in my life to whom I could really open up. Because I was productive—working sixty hours a week—I didn't think I needed an addiction therapist or support group. Yet I could not function well or feel normal without smoking. Cigarettes were moderating my anxiety and levels of tension and helping me to focus. I was using them to celebrate, to give me confidence, to help me cope, and to calm down. If I tried to stop or was even in a place where I was not allowed to smoke for a few hours, I became anxious, restless, volatile, and preoccupied. This was a huge problem that was altering my behavior and personality.

In 1990, when I was thirty-eight, I finally admitted that in many respects my cigarette smoking was as serious and harmful as my mother's alcoholism. Like her, I suffered from depression. Instead of dealing directly with old feelings of distress and loneliness, I was reaching for an escape to keep the negative and painful emotions at bay. That behavior only exacerbated my emptiness and encouraged more escapist habits like eating poorly, not exercising, and being a workaholic. I had been in denial about my dependency on a substance to function on a daily basis for two decades. Not wanting to be a hypocrite, I knew that I had to conquer my compulsion. My patients who quit addictions often said to me, "But it hurts." Instead of trying to take away their discomfort, which I believe is impossible, I counseled them to accept and even to enthusiastically embrace their suffering. It was time to take my own advice.

I realized I wouldn't understand my patients, who I was, or what was going on inside me by pushing my anxiety away with cigarettes. I had to let myself suffer, figure out where it was coming from, and listen to what that pain was trying to tell me. I leaned on an insightful Jungian psychologist and my Adelphi University graduate school mentor, both of whom encouraged me to quit smoking and just let myself feel like hell for an entire year. I needed to get to know what it was inside of me that I had been trying for most of my life to avoid.

Then, long after the physical cravings ceased, I analyzed the support cigarettes had provided. The overwhelming emptiness, hunger, and sadness I finally allowed to surface told me a story about myself that I had never known. It turned out that despite my graduate degrees, professional success, marriage, and bravado, I had never really recovered from the misery of being unloved and unwanted as a child. I had to listen and understand those turbulent feelings I had been fearing and avoiding for so long, or I would never get over my need for nicotine.

Quitting smoking introduced me to the rough, intense, unruly, interior chaos that I feared. Yet instead of aiming to feel better by trying to eradicate those complicated emotions, I understood that I had to learn to live well alongside the agitation and discomfort inside me.

Interestingly, during these difficult twelve months, I came to understand that my mother had felt unwanted by her parents, who had threatened to disown her if she didn't give up her dream of becoming an actress. She had acquiesced to the societal pressures of that era by marrying young and having four children for the wrong reasons and felt stuck in a demanding domestic world that bored her. Perhaps that was the reason she reached for the bottle to cope daily, the way I had latched onto cigarettes.

When the pain of my withdrawal subsided, I was more energized, focused and clear-headed than I had ever been. I could suddenly see that the cigarettes I had been dependent on for more than twenty years had stunted my emotional growth, limited my connections to colleagues, and thwarted intimacy, adversely affecting every area of my existence. Smoking had provided a convenient escape from anxious or ugly emotions. Instead of using strength or creativity to solve my psychological problems and growing wiser, I smoked away the hurt. I saw how counterproductive this had been.

Quitting cigarettes became a catalyst to making other major changes over the next few years. I moved from the suburbs to New York City, launched an exciting private practice, deepened my personal relationships, and learned to turn off my cell phone and preoccupations with work in order to be more present with those I loved. I committed to an addiction-free, conscious, and honest life that revolved around family, healing, and charity.

My experiences helped me form distinct theories on treating addictions, which I taught at Adelphi University, where I completed my doctoral degree, and later at The Village Institute, a Manhattan training clinic I founded in 1995 and expanded to Fayetteville, Arkansas, where I moved in 2005. The method I developed involves an unorthodox blend of behavioral treatments, human connections, and emotional exercises I have used to help thousands of addicts stop smoking, overeating, playing unending video games, watching porn obsessively, sniffing cocaine, drinking a bottle of Jack Daniels every day, and shooting heroin. I was fascinated to learn that all of these very different compulsions—both hard and soft addictions—seem to come from the same desire: to avoid internal darkness.

During the twenty-five years I've now spent working with addicts, I have been inexorably drawn to patients who seem compulsive, enraged, unpredictable, depressed, in pain, and out of control. I can see the beauty in such extremes. It's the same reason I like white-water kayaking. From inside the kayak, the river always starts out looking beautiful and serene. But it is much more violent than it first appears, and ruthless to those who underestimate its strength. Experienced kayakers know that there is always a point, as the kayak moves into the V-shaped rapids, where you cannot turn back or fight where the water wants you to go. No matter how petrified you feel, you have to speed up and head straight into what you fear most. Going forward faster is the only way to attain some element of influence over what the river is about to do to you.

Not long ago, while kayaking in Utah, I almost died. Instead of heading into the rapids, I resisted the river's flow. In a moment of terror, I turned back to the shore, fighting the waves, trying to steer my kayak sideways toward the bank of the river. Panicking, I struggled harder and harder against the current. Then I remembered the fundamental rule every serious kayaker knows. If I fought against the angry white water, I was going to lose. It was absolute; I had no choice. The river was so much stronger than I was. So I stopped resisting. Instead I sped ahead right into the very thing that terrified me, respecting the strength of the hard rapids and humbly hoping the river would cooperate with me. Thankfully, after flipping my kayak upside down, it did. I was bruised and broken, but because I finally submitted to the forces I could not control, despite how fearful I felt, I survived.

This seems an apt metaphor for addiction therapy. Addicts have to accept their powerlessness over their habits. Instead of escaping or fighting or trying to swerve away from what they feel, they must head straight into their emotional pain, which is what terrifies them the most.

I sometimes counter-intuitively tell patients beginning treatment, "Don't trust your instincts, they are always wrong." That's because addicts' feelings, urges, and instincts will always steer them away from turbulence and fear they don't want to face and lead them back to the habits that soothed them. Underlying every substance problem I have ever seen is deep depression that feels unbearable. It is not, in fact, unbearable. But it *feels* like it is. Addicts are often extremely sensitive, overwhelmed by big emotions that can't be smoked, drunk, sniffed, eaten, or gambled away.

The minute they give up their compulsions, they feel raw, agonized, and vulnerable. I warn people in early stages of recovery: You will feel like a burn victim who has no skin. When you go outside, even the air will hurt. This oversensitivity is very common. Thus the AA joke: "When a normal person gets a flat tire, he calls a mechanic. When a recovering addict gets a flat tire, he calls the suicide hotline."

In *Unhooked: How to Quit Anything*, I share my very personal story along with case studies of people who have battled different addictions and won. I offer a simple, step-by-step program showing how you can quit any addiction yourself, or help someone close to you get clean. I start by defining what an addiction is, how it works, and how to tell if a habit is under control or becoming a dangerous problem—if one is "abusing" instead of "using." I chronicle why most addicts depend on substances and not people, thus limiting all intimacy, and suggest places where one can find healthy "core pillars" to lean on when giving up one's unhealthy crutch. Since addicts use substances and activities to regulate emotions, I suggest healthier, more direct, and honest ways of dealing with difficult feelings.

To complete this project, I collaborated with Manhattan author Susan Shapiro, a former patient whom more than a decade ago I helped to quit alcohol and marijuana as well as a twenty-seven-year, two-pack-a-day cigarette habit. To replace her addictions, Susan immersed herself in her passion for writing and has since published seven books, including two about her own experiences in recovery. Amazed at the seemingly-miraculous way this addiction therapy enhanced every aspect of her life, she has been pushing me for years to get all my theories, adages, and directives down in one place.

In *Unhooked* we do not offer false hope or slick promises that giving up a bad habit will be easy. It won't be. There is no magic wand or simple words that can substitute for feeling lousy for a little while. The early stages of transformation can be uncomfortable, awkward, and scary. Many addicts are at first ambivalent about whether it is worth embarking on the difficult journey to quit. That's okay. You can be ambivalent and still make a decision to stop.

Nothing will be more worthwhile, and not only for the reasons you've already heard about improving physical health. What many people don't realize is that substance abuse is often what keeps you from getting what you want most in the world. Along with illuminating the insidious ways an addiction can hurt you and offering steps to stop, *Unhooked* will also help you uncover what's missing from your life and figure out the positive goals and replacements you can reach for—and achieve—instead.

Remember, when you banish a toxic habit from your life, you are making room for something beautiful to take its place.

CHAPTER 1

IS YOUR HABIT ADDICTIVE?: CAFFEINE, WEB SURFING

"Is it possible to be addicted to diet soda?" my co-author, Susan, asked me last year.

"Of course. It's actually a common addiction," I told her.

Susan had lost her voice, and a throat specialist treating her insisted she immediately cease and desist with all the soda she was drinking—even the kind that was caffeine-free. It turned out that she had been consuming ten cans of Diet Coke a day and had immense trouble quitting cold turkey. She couldn't sleep well, work, or concentrate without it.

Susan's personality was so addictive, she could get hooked on carrot sticks. She'd already given up her long term dependency on cigarettes, as well marijuana and alcohol. It's very possible for old addictions to get worse or new habits to pop up, even for a careful recovering addict. In this case, Susan hadn't realized that along with the caffeinated buzz she was relying on daily, she had also become dependent on the chemicals and appetite-squelching effect the diet soda had on her for so many years. Not to mention the soothing rituals of sipping unlimited amounts of the liquid under the illusion that "calorie free" meant healthy. Having to stop yet another substance was more difficult than she expected.

9

"Just when you think you lost everything, you find out that you can always lose a little more," she joked, quoting a post-heart-attack Bob Dylan in *Time Out of Mind*.

Many people assume that an addict only refers to someone who uses hard drugs or excessive alcohol. Yet I define an addiction as a compulsive reliance on *any substance or activity* that harms or deters your ability to function in a major area of your life such as work, school, family, social, and intimate relationships. Often, the substance is used to regulate emotional states that would otherwise feel intolerable if one did not use. A compelling need or desire to use the substance is also present in any addiction, often for no reason that is apparent to the user. Stopping the substance or activity is painful and often seems frightening or impossible.

Obviously a person has to admit to having a problem he or she wants to fix before anything can change. No one can assist someone who is not open to awareness and self-scrutiny. So first ask yourself if you are you ready to come out of denial about your eating, drinking, drug, sex, gambling, or pornography problem. Just because you are not scoring crack in a back alley or chain-smoking forty Marlboros a day does not mean that you do not have an addictive personality type that will eventually gravitate toward damage or destruction. The mild-mannered, clean cut student surfing the web for seven hours a day might be as unhappy, unstable, and lonely as the alcoholic who drinks so much that he winds up arrested or in the hospital.

In some ways the alcoholic might actually be better off than the web surfer because his problem has become obvious, visible, and unarguable. For those afflicted with serious drug habits, services and withdrawal programs are readily available and sponsored by medical establishments, social work clinics, and the government. Yet pretending everything is fine while masking depression with a less overt kind of addiction can be as harmful to your body, soul, and psyche. Less obvious addictions, such as eating, shopping, technology, and gambling disorders, are harder to recognize and identify, and, therefore, individuals who have them are less likely to seek out treatment.

The first step to recovery and to recapturing your full life is to wake up emotionally and examine yourself and your daily rituals in a new way. You can overuse or abuse almost anything. An addiction is something that provides an escape, takes you out of yourself and your day-to-day life, and allows you to get further away from the painful feelings and emotions we would all prefer to avoid. An addiction works short-term but fails miserably long-term because it winds up causing more problems than it solves. Here are the most common areas of abuse that I have seen.

Substances or Activities to Which You Can Easily Become Addicted:

1. Drinking alcohol, including hard liquor, beer, and wine
2. Prescription drugs, including antianxiety medication and painkillers
3. Over-the-counter medications, such as Sudafed, Tylenol, and even aspirin
4. Illegal drugs, including crack, heroin, marijuana, hashish, cocaine, downers, uppers, LSD, and mushrooms
5. Nicotine, including smoking cigarettes and cigars as well as chewing tobacco and even Nicorette gum or spray
6. Pornography, whether it's seen live or in magazines, tapes, movies, television, or on the Internet
7. Gambling, whether it's slot machines in Las Vegas, playing cards, weekly bingo games, or buying lottery tickets
8. Food, including dieting, overeating, anorexia, bulimia, binging, and comfort eating
9. Exercise, which is often associated with eating disorders
10. Adventure sports or high-risk activities, such as white-water rafting and bungee jumping
11. Food and drinks that contain caffeine and other chemicals, including coffee, tea, all kinds of sodas, and chocolate
12. Technology, including television, video games, computer use, email, instant messaging, surfing the web, Facebooking, and tweeting

13. Shopping, even if you can afford what you are buying
14. Working, even if you love your career and need the job to make a living
15. Sex
16. Tattoos and body piercing
17. Cutting yourself and other forms of self-mutilation
18. Celebrity worship, including being a groupie, writing fan letters, stalking, fantasies, and obsessions
19. Cosmetic improvements, including Botox, plastic surgery, hair dye, nail adornments, and makeovers
20. Luxury treatments, such as personal trainers, massages, and going to day spas

THE "HOW TO TELL IF IT'S AN ADDICTION" TEST

Whether it's smoking, drinking, taking drugs, eating junk food, exercising, having sex, gambling, playing video games, or viewing pornography, it's often hard to tell whether one's own habit is healthy, okay in moderation, or a self-destructive addiction that will only get worse. To find out, answer yes or no to the following forty questions. If the answer is maybe or sometimes, count that as a yes.

1. Does doing it lift you out of your day-to-day boredom?
2. Do you use it calm or soothe yourself?
3. Do you feel empty without it?
4. If you go without it for a week, will you feel edgy, anxious, or bored?
5. Does it hurt when you stop?
6. Is it hard to imagine going a long time without it?
7. Have you ever done it to the point of feeling ill or injuring yourself in any way?
8. Has it caused you to do something you regretted and wouldn't have done otherwise?

9. Does stopping cause physical symptoms such as shaking, sweating, or exhaustion?
10. Does it get in the way of your work, school, or primary relationships?
11. Has doing it caused you to flunk a test, drop a class, get reprimanded by a superior, get fired, or otherwise get in the way of school or work?
12. Has it ever ruined a relationship with someone you cared about?
13. Is doing it against the law?
14. Is doing it against your better judgment?
15. Does stopping make you feel depressed, scared, angry, or suicidal?
16. Does doing it ever interfere with your romantic life?
17. Would people in your world be happier if you quit?
18. Do your parents, mate, children, teachers, doctors, or best friend think it's a problem?
19. Are you spending money on it on a regular basis?
20. Are you going into debt because of it?
21. Does it affect your sleep?
22. Would you rather do it than spend time with your mate, family, or friends?
23. Do you prefer to do it alone?
24. Do you ever lie about it or keep it a secret from others?
25. Is getting or doing it an inconvenience to yourself or others?
26. Does it cause you to do irrational things, like spend rent money, go out at four in the morning, or wind up in a dangerous neighborhood?
27. When you do it, is a little not enough?
28. Does your need to do it seem unending?
29. Does it impair your functioning at work, school, home, or social events?
30. Do you need to do it to feel okay at work, school, home, or social events?

31. Do you ever crave it when you're not doing it?
32. Do you need it regularly?
33. Do you have anxiety when people in your life bring it up or ask about your habit?
34. Do other family members have the same habit?
35. Do you look forward to doing it?
36. Have you tried to stop and failed?
37. Do you think it's a problem?
38. Do you think your life would be better if you stopped doing it?
39. Do you regret that you can't stop?
40. Does your brain tell you that you would feel better if you quit?

SCORING:

If you have answered yes to more than five of these questions, your habit is on the way to becoming an addiction. It is already starting to negatively interfere with other areas of your life. The chances are that without treatment or intervention it will get worse.

When it came to diet soda, Susan answered yes to ten of the "How to Tell If It's an Addiction" questions. She admitted that along with her throat specialist, her gynecologist and an oncologist she'd once seen had both warned her about negative effects of so much diet soda. Her dentist couldn't bleach her dark, soda-stained teeth. After a root canal, the endodontist warned her that the ingredients in soda eroded tooth enamel, making emergency procedures more likely. She decided it was time to bid diet soda adieu.

Susan felt bereft and uncomfortable for three months, shocked that such a legal, cheap, ubiquitous liquid had such a hold on her. Now she drinks only water (which she sometimes sips through a straw in an empty Diet Coke can) and tea, to which she was adding too much honey and subsequently also had to quit. (It's actually rare when an addict only has one addiction, something I discuss in depth in a later chapter on avoiding the "substance shuffle.")

But the point here is that yes, one can get addicted to pedestrian, strange, and seemingly innocuous substances and activities. The first thing you need to do is become more conscious of your habits and make a decision that it's time to cut down or quit.

Ways to Tell if Your Habit is Becoming an Addiction:

1. **TAKE INVENTORY:** Pay careful attention to all of your habits and activities. Are you sleeping through the night? Are you feeling well rested, well fed, and in shape? Do you notice how much you are eating, drinking, and spending? Is there any illegal or unethical dilemmas that are bothering you (like drugs, debts, or infidelity)? Are there any recent changes you find troubling? If you had to give up one substance or activity, what would it be?

2. **TRY TO QUIT COLD TURKEY:** If you are so positive that your drinking, smoking, eating, gambling, shopping, or penchant for a little pornography is not really a big deal, then go one week without it—starting from when you wake up tomorrow morning. If you find it easy to be clean for seven days straight, then maybe you do not have an addiction. On the other hand, if you cannot get out of bed, or if you feel depressed, angry, anxious, scared, paranoid, or edgy without using—or if you find yourself really missing your substance—it is probably time to face your problem.

3. **FIGURE OUT WHAT YOU ARE FEELING IN THE MOMENT YOU REACH FOR YOUR HABIT:** The minute you speak to your mother on the phone long distance, do you light up a cigarette? After leaving a meeting with your boss, do you immediately reach for a donut? Does feeling nervous and awkward at a party make you want a beer or glass of wine to chill out? See if there is a correlation between uncomfortable emotions and your habits. Regulating your feelings by using an activity or substance is rarely a healthy way to cope. It usually indicates that the substance you are using is either an addiction or on its way to becoming an addiction and needs to be seriously reconsidered.

4. **DO THE MATH:** While some bad habits are free, most of them (like cigarettes, alcohol, drugs, and gambling) can adversely affect your bank account quickly. So figure out exactly how much you are consuming and spending on your habit. Compare this to what you earn and what you'd rather be purchasing.

   For example, Susan figured out she was actually spending $10 a day on Diet Coke, which added up to $3,750 annually. She had been drinking diet soda since she was thirteen years old. By switching to water, she could get her voice back, be healthier, and save an awful lot of money.

   When she first came to see me in the 1990s, Susan was a two-pack-a-day smoker who also used marijuana regularly and drank at bars and social events. She figured out that she was spending at least $3,000 a year on cigarettes, $1,200 on pot, and $1,200 on drinks, which added up to $5,400. Her income was $24,000 the previous year, so she was unknowingly spending almost one fourth of her salary on her habits. She said she could not afford therapy ($125 a session at that point) or a freelance editor for a book she wrote but had not been able to sell ($2,000). When she added it all up, the solution seemed obvious. She decided to use both therapy and the freelance editor, quit all three habits, and published three books the next year, tripling her income.

5. **ATTEND ONE SESSION OF AN ADDICTION GROUP:** Many studies have shown that involvement in any addiction-recovery group correlates with higher chances of staying clean and sober. So force yourself to go to one meeting for Alcoholics Anonymous, Narcotics, Gamblers, Debtors Anonymous, Overeaters Anonymous, or Weight Watchers. You do not have to ever go back or say anything out loud, but require yourself to sit through an entire meeting without making any judgments. Afterwards, how do you feel? Have you recognized some of the stories that members shared? Have you identified with anyone? You do not need to make a long-term commitment to benefit from

attending a group. They are mostly free or low cost so you have nothing to lose (but your bad habit).

6. **ASK YOUR MEDICAL DOCTOR FOR DATA:** If you smoke or toke, find out how much damage you have already done to your lungs. If you drink, ask your doctor what effect alcohol is having on your body. If your problem is food, your doctor might be able to provide information on the medical consequences of obesity. If you have been bulimic or anorexic, find out the potential consequences of purging or starving your body and the statistics on how many people wind up hospitalized from food disorders every year. Getting the full picture might scare you straight or at least into admitting that your self-destructive actions could threaten your physical health.

7. **SEE AN ADDICTION PROFESSIONAL:** Commit to one talk-therapy appointment to discuss your concerns with a substance-abuse specialist, counselor, local psychiatrist, psychologist, social worker, or sponsor who is familiar with addictions. One appointment might cost you anywhere from $50 to $200, but it will be worth it to step up and to find out if you have a problem before it ruins your marriage, bank account, career, children, and life. An addiction specialist can walk you through all these steps and suggest more extensive, idiosyncratic solutions that fit your personality, along with providing emotional support. In my experience, people who are willing to go for therapy, as well as regularly attending an addiction group, recover more often than anyone else.

8. **ASK PEOPLE YOU TRUST:** One at a time, approach friends, colleagues, doctors, or loved ones, tell them you need their honest and discreet opinion on a private matter and ask, "Do you think the way that I drink (or smoke, eat, exercise, gamble, shop) is a problem?" After you ask, you are not allowed to speak. Just listen to their answer. If people who care about you express concern, chances are this problem does not exist only in your imagination and should be addressed before it gets worse.

9. **ASK A FORMER USER:** Most addicts who have quit bad habits or are in an AA-type group are very proud of having stopped. At a private moment, ask to speak to some such person and confide that you were wondering if you might have issues with substance abuse. He or she might recognize your symptoms or early warning signals and offer to share his or her strategy or hard-earned wisdom.

10. **DOES IT INVOLVE SECRETS, DECEPTIONS, AND LIES:** There is a difference between overeating at a family dinner and sneaking junk food by yourself at three in the morning. When you pig out alone on a continual basis, it might somehow imply that you think what are you doing is bad or shameful. Whatever your habit is, do you only do it when you are by yourself? Hiding or lying about it if someone asks could be one mark that it's become an addiction.

CHAPTER 2

WRITE TO FIND OUT WHAT YOU THINK: ANOREXIA, SOCIAL FUNCTIONS & DYSFUNCTIONS

Can you get addicted to church functions? I learned the answer when Jean, who said she was "a church-going Catholic wife and mother" came to see me about her anorexic daughter, Stacey. It seemed the whirlwind of religious activity at the center of Jean's life had left Stacey feeling so completely alone and alienated that she had rejected all food.

While treating patients with eating disorders in the past, I learned that anorexia is a compulsive, harmful activity used for numbing and controlling internal feelings, which fit my criteria for labeling it as an addiction. I agreed to meet Stacey.

There was only one problem. During my first four months of treatment with her, she did not say one word to me the entire time.

Stacey was a sixteen-year-old redheaded girl who, at five foot three and seventy pounds, had been hospitalized numerous times and was fed intravenously. She hadn't menstruated in two years and her immune system was so frail that, according to her doctor, even getting the flu could kill her. By the time she came to my Arkansas office in the spring of 2009, Stacey was emaciated and on the verge of death. She was living at home with her parents, who brought Stacey in to see me. Stacey agreed to therapy simply because her parents had given her no choice. It was me or the hospital, which she dreaded the most. However, once she came to my office, she just sat there mute, refusing to speak.

In our first session, I asked her parents to accompany her for the first ten minutes to explain to me (and Stacey) their motivation for bringing her to see me. But after I asked her mother and father to leave, Stacey still did not say one word. She sat with her head down, numb and unresponsive. When she subsequently came in for solo appointments, she remained quiet. As in total silence. Week after week. In thirty years of practice, this had never happened to me before.

Stacey looked so lost and expressionless I did not sense that she was playing a game or trying to challenge me. It was as if she had no voice, no energy, no will to live. I had felt hopeless and forlorn myself throughout my childhood, wishing somebody would have been concerned or interested enough to fight through my shield of darkness. I had a teenage daughter just a few years younger. What if my little girl was in that much pain? I desperately wanted to reach Stacey. So each session, I would talk to her, nonstop.

"Your parents said other therapists and doctors in the past have failed you. I think it's because they were obsessed with your food issues, so I'm not going to focus on them. I'm not here to treat your anorexia. For now, I'm here to treat your psyche and your soul, where the real problems are. Okay?" I asked, pretending we were having a two-sided conversation. If someone had been watching the scene, I'm sure my hour-long monologues filled with my exaggerated hand gestures, unanswered questions, and personal stories about my own struggles might have looked ridiculous. But I was committed to connecting with this girl. Based on my luck with previous difficult cases, I felt that sharing my own troubled history would be a way to find her.

During her four months of silence, I told Stacey all about the shrinks who had treated and disappointed me in the past, what I'd learned from these failures, and how I wanted to provide for my patients the help that therapy had at first failed to give to me. I let her know that I could empathize with the hopelessness and anguish I guessed she was feeling because I had a mother who never loved me and had wished me dead. I related my belief that life could be brutal and unfair, chronicling how my Battery Park City townhouse was severely damaged and taken away from me in the World Trade Center attacks on 9/11 and how that led me to move my family to Arkansas. Many therapists prefer a more reserved, blank-slate approach. I have no problem sharing details of my personal life with patients if I believe it might help them.

Although Stacey did not respond with words, I could detect small movements in her eyebrows and changes in the way her blue eyes followed me when I stood up to get a glass of water. Sometimes she'd lean forward slightly and I could feel her engagement. Other times she would look away distracted and I'd say "Uh oh, I've lost you." Then she would turn back to me. I knew she was listening, and I hoped I was slowly getting through.

"It doesn't matter if you don't speak to me for years. I will keep talking and cure you anyway," I told her. "If you think not answering will make me stop, you're wrong. Because I'm never going to shut up or give up on you."

People in my profession are often taught to ask questions instead of make statements, to sound neutral instead of opinionated, to say things like, "Perhaps you might consider the possibility that . . ." I, too, was trained to be accepting and nonjudgmental and never say anything to a patient that sounds arrogant, provocative, or critical. But that's not the kind of therapy that helped me, and it's not the kind of therapist I want to be. I cannot think of any other profession in which an expert never criticizes, fears value judgments, won't make strong statements, or offer concise decisions. A professional with intelligence and personality in any other field is allowed and expected to be firm and resolute. Imagine if you went to a surgeon who constantly equivocated and was apprehensive about making a clear diagnosis or even share an opinion. Or you let a fireman into your burning house who then hemmed and hawed, uncertain whether to run upstairs or call for backup, asking "How do *you* feel about it?"

Many addicts I've treated, like Stacey, face life or death situations. Patients could die from starvation or an overdose or drive drunk or take drugs in front of their children, causing all kinds of irreparable damage to themselves or their family. Often an addict's instincts for self-preservation have stopped functioning and, like Stacey, he needs to hear a voice powerful enough to combat an addictive impulse. I believe that sometimes addicts feel safer, reassured, and in better hands with a strong authority figure offering clear direction. Some people come to see me as a last resort after all else has failed. They pay for my opinion and expertise. My goal is to provide immediate assistance. I don't mind going out on a limb, or being seen as overconfident or aggressive, if I think doing so might save someone's life.

After four months, at our fifteenth session, expounding on the deep despair I felt when I was Stacey's age, I said, "I'm sure you don't have a clue what I'm talking about."

"Yes, I do," she said quietly.

I laughed and said, "Oh, she talks," trying to make light of it, not wanting her to feel self-conscious. She smiled. After that, she talked more and more. Only then did I shut up and listen.

Gradually Stacey spoke of her deep depression and despair. She was sure she did not deserve to exist. She felt unheard and unseen. Nobody knew her. She said she was cold, numb, lost in herself. She loved school; it was the only thing that mattered to her. But she felt the compulsion to get perfect grades and had no real friends there. She said she was all alone in the world; even God had forsaken her. She was sure she would never belong. She felt guilty, ugly, and bad, and believed that the smaller she was and the less space she took up, the less offensive she would be to God and the universe.

I asked Stacey to start a journal about what she was feeling so she could continue our intimate dialogue outside of our sessions. It was much easier for her to write her emotions than to speak about them.

After a few more months, she started emailing me poetic pages that she had typed into her laptop. About a trip with her mother to the mountains, she wrote: "As my exhausted eyes scanned the coming winter-time . . . these shadows of hills and comfortless sky shoved its heavy body against mine as a reminder of the absurd futility of hoping . . . I had no idea what the future held, as I had hoped to die before then . . ."

Stacey had not yet been able to verbalize to me that she was suicidal or say the words "I hoped to die." Sending me this passage to read was a breakthrough. By letting me know, she was helping me to help her. It gave me hope she would not die. I was relieved. Stacey said she'd never admitted any of this to anyone before—even herself. Her journal allowed us both to better understand her fragility and how much work we still had to do. I began printing out some of the pages and asked her to read them aloud to me in sessions so we could both hear the words coming from her. At first she shook her head, no. I had to push and cajole her to do so. "Come on, please. I really want to hear you read it." Finally she acquiesced. Her voice was small, hesitant, self-conscious, afraid—as if she had no right to put her presence into the world with speech.

I was fascinated by the way Stacey now described her feelings during all of our sessions when she had been mute: "I have been betrayed by doctors and therapists who treated me by the book rather than as a human. I felt like a problem to be fixed, like someone not fully under the effect of anesthesia, unable to speak, yet still able to feel the knife . . . The beginning with Dr. Woolverton was the same as with all therapists. But he didn't probe me the way the others had . . . He kept talking about himself. He made me feel connected . . . Despite my silence, he remained convinced in his ability to help me . . . I disregarded my reservations and decided I would do whatever he asked. If life proved to be too much I could always kill myself. I took a leap of faith and trusted him."

I was grateful she did. But I also knew the limitations of trying to help a patient one hour once a week. Stacey's survival depended on expanding her trust to others who could be there for her around the clock. A recurring theme in her sessions and her journal was that her mother didn't get her or see her or love her. Although Stacey knew I met with both of her parents periodically to discuss her life-threatening condition, after two more months, I suggested working with Stacey and her mother together. Stacey said no, it was pointless since she had no hope that her mom could ever understand her. But she agreed to let me treat her mother alone; Stacey seemed neutral about it and showed no discomfort. When I asked further, she said it was hopeless, but gave me her permission, saying, "Good luck." She was totally alienated from her mother. Her attitude was, "Sure, see what you can do with her."

Unlike many therapists who adhere to a doctrine against treating members of the same family or seeing two partners separately, I don't have absolute rules on the subject. Interestingly, neither did Sigmund Freud, the father of psychoanalysis. Indeed, Freud invited his patients to his house for dinner and introduced them to his family. It was the post-Freudians who imposed stringent rules on treatment. As controversial as some of my practices are in some circles, I believe good addiction therapy mixes psychoanalytic and behavioral methods. I don't care if they are considered unorthodox if they help patients. My priority is to get addicts off dangerous drugs and stop activities that could be fatal, or cause damage to themselves, their spouses, and children. So I assess what is needed differently in each case.

Sometimes a mother, father, or a spouse is the only one who can provide my patient with the care or support they need on a day-to-day basis. It can be incredibly illuminating to meet a child and parent, or two partners, one-on-one. Although I realize it might be risky, it is sometimes easier for me to assist when I hear the whole story from a perspective that is different from the addict's, which allows me to help two parties work better together.

When Stacey's mother, Jean, first came in, she smiled widely and said, "It's so nice to meet you. It's such a pleasure to be here. I've heard so much about all the great work you do to help people at The Village Institute." She was a pretty, perky, middle-class, Irish Catholic, forty-two-year-old redhead who was sharing small talk as if we were meeting at a party. Given the grave danger her daughter was in, her sociable, courteous mask was troubling. Jean was wearing so many layers of politeness she could barely admit why she was in my office. After I had started seeing Stacey weekly, I was especially dismayed when I realized that Jean might have continued her superficial chatter for the entire session if I did not stop her.

"What beautiful weather we're having," she once began.

"Look, Jean, you need to put all the niceties aside and face the horrible things that are happening to your family," I told her.

She started to cry.

"Tell me why you're crying," I asked.

"Stacey isn't in such good shape."

"For the last two years your daughter has been close to death. If you want to help Stacey you have to stop smiling and complimenting me and start talking honestly about what is really going on."

It was not my intention to be hurtful, but I needed to be forceful to wake her up. I wanted Jean to understand what I knew. I always make it clear to my patients that I am going to be an active participant in the treatment. No lies, no games. I speak my mind and don't waste time. I want to relay what I am hearing and thinking. I never think therapy should be a polite encounter. I agree with the Austrian-born psychoanalyst, Melanie Klein, who believed that a therapist can say anything at all to a patient. It is not what you say but how you say it that counts. I usually try to balance my candor with sufficient gentleness and concern so I don't shock or alienate anyone I want to assist. Yet, since Stacey weighed less than 100 pounds and I feared she could still wind up dead, I was willing to risk rudeness with her mother.

"I don't know why Stacey is sick. We love her so much. I did my best. We always went to church together. She was so happy growing up," Jean told me.

"Apparently that really wasn't the whole story," I insisted.

"I just don't understand what's wrong," Jean said, sobbing. I handed her a tissue.

Jean told me how her husband, Tom, an airline pilot, was often away, and her eighteen-year-old daughter, Rachel, was a college theater student who had recently moved into her own apartment. (Rachel appeared to have no eating issues.) Jean was lonely and her way of dealing with the loneliness was by going out and socializing. All the time. She called herself "a social butterfly," which was an understatement. I soon ascertained that Jean's existence revolved around attending religious services every Wednesday and Sunday, along with church functions, fund-raisers, mixers, committee meetings, charity lunches and dinners—almost every day and night. She was hardly ever home and hadn't been in years.

Although I often encourage patients to get involved in religious activities, Jean hadn't realized her social life had become a harmful addiction contributing to her daughter's illness and tearing her family apart.

"We have a good life. We're blessed. We have a nice house, cars, enough money, everything we ever wanted," Jean went on. "Can you tell me what's hurting Stacey?"

"You are a good person with a good heart," I told her, honestly. "But you keep yourself so constantly busy that you don't have time to know how your daughter feels or how you feel."

"I'm trying to help her," Jean said.

"Aren't you sad that your husband is away so much?"

"That's just his job," she answered. "He's a good man and a good provider."

I realized I was going to have to cut to the chase.

"Your daughter wants to die. How does that make you feel?"

Jean cried again. I saw that she was so used to having superficial, upbeat, phony conversations with acquaintances, she didn't know what was really going on under the surface. Church socials and charity functions are ostensibly positive activities. Yet in this case, Jean was subconsciously using them to get away from sadness and from dealing with darker problems. It took her three sessions to admit that she actually hated being without her husband so often but had never once told him—or herself—that truth.

For years she'd been awash in loneliness. She had no career. Her older daughter was independent and didn't need her anymore. Stacey was slipping away. Jean loved her family but nobody was intimately connected. Her social life was a dangerous addiction because it was interfering with her marriage and child's health. It existed mostly so she could get away from what she was feeling inside. If she stopped, she would hurt. She rationalized that anything connected with religion was good. But too much of something healthy (even drinking too much water!) can become a big problem, especially if you remain unaware of what is motivating the activity. Jean was scared of being quiet and alone because then all of her unhappiness and fears about her daughter would surface.

Of course Stacey's illness was devastating to her. Yet to help in her recovery, Jean first had to recognize her own problem: she was making nightly plans and overscheduling all of her days in order to not feel bad. Once she identified this problem, she had to identify the consequences. She didn't really know her children—one of whom was near death. She didn't know herself. She was numb, locked in a social pattern that would keep her empty.

As I sometimes do at the start of therapy, I suggested Jean begin writing down what was really going on and upsetting her. She needed to acknowledge and give voice to her darkest feelings the way Stacey had learned to do. Jean had never expressed how she felt. She had to figure this out so that she could stop running around in a mindless whirlwind and finally find out who her daughter was and how to help her get better.

"I always wanted to write," she admitted.

"Write! Express yourself! Don't hold back anything," I told her. "You don't have to show it to me or anybody."

Within the next few weeks Jean returned with many pages she had printed out from her computer that she wanted to share with me. "I feel all the good I've done has been a cover for how bad I feel inside. I've been lonely and alone my entire life," she confessed. "I wonder why I am crying right now. I am crying tears that have wanted to be cried for many years." Like her daughter, the process of journaling allowed her to tap into a deeper level of feeling than she'd been able to verbalize before.

Jean wrote for an hour early every single morning. She was soon able to express frustration with her husband and the job that kept him away from her. She wrote how religion had been her only way to order the universe and reassure herself that she was a good person. But now she felt misled by the clergy who had promised her that if she prayed, came to church, and was a good person who didn't lie or steal, everything would be fine. Obviously—with a daughter literally starving herself to death—everything was far from fine. While religious doctrine could offer a fine, moralistic blueprint to live by, it could not take the place of family closeness or fix every problem.

Jean soon realized she felt let down by her own parents who had never held her or said they loved her. She felt she had to be a straight-A, churchgoing, good little girl with poise and excellent manners. She feared her mother and father had never known her for who she really was and that she had re-created that idealistic, yet empty pattern with her children.

The more Jean wrote about what she was feeling and lived with her feelings, the less she needed to go out. With many addicts, social life is an essential component of recovery and I encourage it. Yet in Jean's case, with a sick daughter and semiabsent husband, the church activities (everything from the services to the prayers to the community it provided) had actually *become* the addiction that was detrimental to the health of her kin. Jean admitted she wasn't going out for intimacy or spiritual connection or even fun. It was an escape. She needed to find ways to be home more and to be more intimate with her family.

As the months went by, Jean emailed me sections of her journal, and we talked about them when she came in. "I keep trying to imagine the horrors that my daughter must feel to be doing this to herself and her life. I blame myself," she read to me. This was excruciating for her to admit because she had tried to be such a perfect mother.

Although I encouraged Jean to be honest and self-critical, too much blaming of herself was counterproductive. If all she did was walk around feeling guilty, she wouldn't be empathetic to Stacey and would continue to miss her daughter. I often find parental guilt is unproductive, especially when what is needed is action, compassion, and empathy. Based on my own difficulties, even at the age of fifty-nine, trying to reconnect with my mother, I believe it's never too late to fix the mother-child bond.

With challenging cases, I often think of Melanie Klein's psychoanalytical theory: when a mother is not loving or protective enough, her child experiences extreme anxiety, dread, or terror of being utterly alone and abandoned. Consider all the maternal metaphors attached to addiction: Alcoholics are "on the bottle." Smokers inhale deeply, the way a baby sucks milk from a breast. If you ever watch a smoker who has not had a cigarette in a while finally light up, or a heroin addict nod out from a fix, you'll see how it resembles a hungry infant nursing. The addict gets filled up, his or her whole body seems warm, quenched, smoothed, and transformed. Listen to gamblers as they kiss the dice, or right before the dealer turns over a card: "Come on, momma, smile on me," they'll say. "I know you love me. You're gonna make me a winner." If Lady Luck shines on you, everything is going to be just fine. Is it any surprise that many people (like me) have tried to comfort themselves with a treat of ice cream—made up of milk and sugar—right before they go to sleep?

In Stacey's case, I wondered if the story behind her refusing food revealed that she had no idea how to take in her mother's love. Since dropping so much weight caused this sixteen-year-old to lose her breasts and hips and stop getting her period, perhaps anorexia symbolized Stacey's rejection of everything involving femininity and motherhood. Yet, since Jean's intentions were good and she was deeply affected by Stacey's plight and willing to do anything she could to keep her daughter alive, I focused on helping Jean reconstruct her relationship with her daughter.

"Stacey doesn't believe you really love her, want to know her, or can handle the truth," I said. I advised Jean that instead of *telling* Stacey how great their life was, she had to start *asking* Stacey, "What's wrong?" Then she had to really listen, without interrupting or interjecting religious commentary, advice, or stories about herself. "Just make it all about Stacey and take in what she's saying and feeling," I instructed. "If you want to argue or defend yourself, do that with me, or in your journal. I know it seems unfair, but Stacey's still in danger." To speed up the healing process, Jean needed to give the unconditional love, support, and attention to her daughter that Stacey felt she'd never had.

Jean brought in her husband, Tom, again. He was five years older than his wife, a distinguished-looking man with gray hair. At first he seemed conservative, inhibited, and emotionally stoic. But soon I saw it was just a facade. Tom wanted to go deeper, he just didn't know how to get there, or what to do or say. "How do you feel about what's going on with your family?" I asked him.

"I'm mystified by what's hurting Stacey," he told me. "We loved her and took care of her. Where did we go wrong?"

"That's the mystery we're here to unravel," I told him. "Opening up and talking about what's really happening is the first step."

He looked completely exhausted. When I asked if he was getting enough sleep, I learned that he had taken it upon himself to sit by Stacey's bedside to make sure she drank two full glasses of a protein shake daily. Some nights it took her four or five hours to drink one. It wasn't a physical limitation, it was emotional. She was so hesitant and afraid to get any nutrients inside her that it had become a torturous routine. Tom would stay up past midnight waiting, and then had to leave for work at five in the morning. He was so tired, he said, he once fell asleep at the wheel of his car driving to work.

"If you die in a car crash, Stacey will have no chance of recovery," I told him. "Tell her tomorrow you can't risk dying in a traffic accident or killing your passengers because you are too tired. She has one hour to drink the shake. If she says no, tell her that the consequences of her decision will be that she cannot go to school." I knew school was what Stacey cared about most, and, sure enough, she started finishing her drink within the allotted time.

After a few sessions together, when Tom said, "I love my wife," Jean interrupted to say, "Then why don't you ever show it?"

I encouraged her to keep sharing her feelings with him, even if it was difficult to talk about. "I am lonely. I don't want to be lonely anymore," she was finally able to say.

Tom was at first perplexed. "I work so hard. I've always been loyal and faithful."

"You are. But I'm still lonely," Jean said.

"I'm so good to my family. I buy them everything they need," he argued.

"Fidelity and financial support are not enough," I explained. "Even when you travel for work, you have to be there for them emotionally. You have to help your wife to not feel lonely."

They had met and fallen in love at a small southern college, but had no real tools or language with which to communicate any kind of pain or discomfort. After Jean learned to express to him what was hurting her and what she needed that she wasn't getting, I suggested new rules. When Tom was away on business, he had to call Jean and talk on the phone for half an hour every night, or preferably by Skype so they could see each other, no matter where he was.

"What should we talk about?" he asked.

"Ask her how she feels. How her day went. When she misses you the most," I suggested.

Although they were awkward at first, Jean appreciated that Tom was making the effort, which gave her hope. She soon stopped feeling obligated to sound perky and happy and instead understood how important it was for her to share negative, uncomfortable emotions, too. When he was back in town, they took hour-long walks. It had been so long since they had showed physical affection, they had to practice holding hands walking down the street. I suggested they sit and read books together in the same room at night.

Jean began to make much more time to be with Stacey. Sometimes they would get into Jean's silver Honda and just drive around with no destination, listening to Stacey's favorite music: CDs by Animal Collective, Fleet Foxes, and TV on the Radio—eclectic soulful alternative rock and folk that grew on Jean. It wasn't the activity that mattered, but the time she was sharing with her daughter. They had always been so busy "doing the right thing" that Stacey had never felt like she was at the center of her parents' love or attention. The important rule I made was that it had to be Stacey's choice and that Jean's taste, desires, and religious agenda no longer counted. During Stacey's recovery, it had to be only about her. Sometimes they went shopping, took a walk, or went to movies. They started cooking dinners together although Stacey still refused to eat in front of anyone.

Stacey could tell that her mother was trying hard to open up and appreciated the effort, even if it was clumsy. When they drove around together, not talking, but just listening to music Stacey liked, Stacey felt the closest to her mom. "She's really trying, isn't she?" Stacey recently asked me, albeit with a tone of cynicism.

After two years, Stacey moved into an apartment with a roommate near her parents. She is currently applying to liberal arts colleges. Stacey now weighs 105 pounds—thirty-five pounds more than when I first met her. The chart says for her height she should weigh closer to 120, but she's menstruating again and in the realm of normal weight.

Jean continues monthly therapy sessions with me, either alone or with her husband. They go to a few church functions together. But she needed a new activity that meant something special just for her, and she decided to take a creative writing class. There she befriended an author working on a book with an anorexic character, and they spent time talking about what living with someone who has anorexia is like. Jean is still chronicling her loneliness, anger, and disappointment, which is a good sign. If she were writing about how happy she was, I would know she'd had a relapse.

I find writing to be a great way for addicts to learn to connect their external habits to what is going on inside them, to express words that are too uncomfortable or confusing to speak. As Joan Didion said, "I write to find out what I think." Along with journaling or keeping a diary, there are many other creative methods where you can learn to let out deeper feelings. I've treated people who have painted, sculpted, taken photographs, played music, or written songs. One patient would sing along with lyrics to old songs from her past that made her sad and let herself cry. If you don't find a comfortable home for these emotions, they get cast away and that essential part of yourself gets lost, buried, and never heard. This repression has a negative, cumulative effect, and, as in the case of Jean and Stacey, it can explode, sometimes too late.

Stacey has yet to show anything she's written to her mother. Yet Jean printed out pages from her journal and gave them to her daughter. Right there on the spot, Stacey read about her mother's pain, worry, and loneliness. She was fascinated and surprised by how deep and dark the sentiments were. She had no idea her mother had hidden all these feelings and asked to read more.

HOW TO START STOPPING

To quit an addiction, I highly recommend that you—like Jean and Stacey—start writing every day, whether it's in a journal, a loose-leaf notebook, a desktop computer, or an iPad. Jot down your feelings, your food or drug intake, your plans, or poems, songs, or adages you like. Get specific about your habits. Instead of identifying "smoking," admit that you've "smoked a pack a day of Marlboros for twenty years" and all the methods you've tried to quit in the past.

"Overeating" is too general; emulate the novel *Bridget Jones' Diary* and detail: "pigged out on cookies at 2:00 AM again." Here are some other ways to begin the process of quitting.

1. **DECIDE NOW IS THE TIME TO GET CLEAN:** Realize—and verbalize—that you want to stop altering your emotional state with an addiction. You can be scared, anxious, cynical, or ambivalent and still make this decision.

2. **FIND WHAT'S MISSING:** Figure out what you want most in your life that you haven't been able to get. Can you make a list of exactly what that is? Sometimes, as an exercise, I recommend writing your fantasy obituary to get in touch with what you hope your life accomplishments will be. Acknowledge that your addiction is probably what's been standing in your way of getting what you need most deeply. And admit that it is a poor substitute.

3. **DON'T BE AN I-LAND:** Realize that no one can quit an addiction alone. As you'll read in the next two chapters, you'll need "core pillars" who are willing to help. As a first step, try to find an addiction mentor—preferably someone who has been on the wagon that you can check in with regularly, whether in person, by phone, Skype, Facebook, or email.

4. **UPON THE MOMENT OF COMMITMENT, THE WORLD WILL HELP YOU:** Research available resources. Google "addiction services" and your state, go to the library, check out addiction sections of a bookstore, make calls to your school—which often provides free drug counseling—and review your medical insurance, which may cover addiction therapy.

5. **VISIT YOUR DOCTOR:** Consider seeing a physician to find out if there's medicine that can help you. Heroin addicts often benefit from methadone treatment. Many smokers quit easier with the nicotine patch, gum, or inhaler. Often treating your ADD, ADHD, chronic pain, anxiety, or depression with a prescription for an appropriate medication makes quitting the addiction much easier.

6. **MAKE AN APPOINTMENT:** Try to go to one recovery meeting or have a one-on-one session with an addiction specialist, a drug counselor, or a friend who had similar problems they've stopped. If you want to quit an addiction, take steps to find a method that will work for you.

7. **PUT TOGETHER A PLAN:** This can involve spending a month in rehab, attending daily meetings, committing to weekly therapy, joining Weight Watchers, getting the nicotine patch, or walking three times a week with a friend. The more healthy substitutes, the better your chances of quitting for good.

8. **DESIGNATE D-DAY:** It could be your birthday, your child's birthday, or an arbitrary date. I recommend you avoid New Year's Day (for reasons later discussed).

9. **SLOW DOWN:** Sleeplessness, stress, workaholism, and over-scheduling exacerbate addictive behavior. Transformations that stick require time, thoughtfulness, energy, and introspection. If possible, take vacation days, a holiday, or a weekend off. If you can't, consider a yoga class, meditation, a long massage, or an afternoon by yourself with no obligations or deadlines. You need time to think, relax, breathe, and rationally assess where you are emotionally and where you need to go next.

10. **BE OPEN-MINDED:** Yes, you've been running your life, love, work, sleep, meal plan, and exercise regime in a certain way for many years. Patterns are hard to break. But you might have to re-evaluate everything you do and consume to uncover where the problem really lies. Something as seemingly minor as going to sleep an hour earlier, waking up a bit later, saying no to a social event, switching from soda to tea, or adding another night with childcare to your schedule can make the difference between failure and success.

11. **PREPARE TO FEEL LIKE HELL:** Do not expect to quit and feel better. It does not work that way. When you quit, you will at first feel worse. Yet, through feeling worse you will be entering a life that is deeper, more interesting, and more intense than anything

you have felt up until now. Once you give yourself permission to suffer and be sad, you have already lessened the suffering you will go through because it won't take you by surprise. You will be more prepared for the inevitable withdrawal symptoms. There are many ways I will recommend on how to "suffer well."

12. **KNOW YOUR EMOTIONS & MOOD SWINGS WON'T MAKE SENSE:** Don't wait to be ready to quit. No one ever is. When you stop, it might feel like the worst decision you could have made. These feelings are inevitable. But feelings are not facts. I will discuss why feelings misinform and often lead you to continue self-destructive habits. The only way to change is to change; understanding follows.

CHAPTER 3

LEARN TO RELY ON PEOPLE, NOT SUBSTANCES: CIGARETTES, ALCOHOL, SUGAR

Many people who have watched the television shows *Breaking Bad*, *Weeds*, *Rescue Me*, *Huge*, *My Name is Earl*, *Two and a Half Men* and such reality shows as *Big Life*, *The Biggest Loser*, and *Dr. Drew's Celebrity Rehab* buy into the misconception that addicts are somehow funny, charming, cool, and entertaining. Nothing could be further from the truth. Being addicted is a serious, painful, and sad problem that can ruin your life—and innocent people in your path. The nation was shocked and horrified recently when an unemployed army veteran, David Laffer, shot and killed four people at a Medford, New York, pharmacy where he went to steal pain medication for his wife.

Given the statistics, it's actually more surprising that these kinds of tragedies don't happen more often. Indeed, recent studies indicate that drug addiction currently afflicts more than 10,000,000 people and since 1990, the number of individuals who take prescription drugs illegally is believed to have risen over 500 percent. Twenty-two million Americans are alcoholics. At least 60,000,000 in our country are obese. Despite the obvious links to lung cancer, 20 percent of

United States citizens still regularly smoke cigarettes. Eight million are diagnosed "shopaholics." If you add gambling, pornography, caffeine, television and video game addictions, computer compulsions, and workaholism, it becomes clear that the use of substances that control emotional states is a widespread phenomenon. Drug and alcohol abuse kills people and perpetuates crime, destruction, violence, and fatal automobile accidents. Obese patients suffer from medical problems that lead to 400,000 deaths a year—the same amount who die from smoking-related illnesses.

I have helped patients cease shooting cocaine and heroin into their veins, quit drinking a whole bottle of Jack Daniels a day, hand over weapons, halt habitually smoking crack, marijuana, and hashish, and quit popping pills, along with stopping lying, stealing, and selling sex in order to pay for their habits. I have watched individuals give up smoking three packs of cigarettes a day, filling their lungs with poison, and quit spending or gambling away money they needed for their rent, food, or children's education. I have assisted others stem their abuse of food through excessive eating, dieting, anorexia, bulimia, binging, and overexercising. I have treated males and females from the ages of fourteen to seventy-five, ranging from a highly functioning, successful attorney to a violent and down-and-out drunk threatening to hurt himself and other people.

Addictions come in many different forms and afflict people of all races, religions, backgrounds, ages, and classes. Even well-adjusted, well-respected, law abiding citizens who never smoke, drink, or take drugs are not exempt from the nightmare of substance abuse. An accident, death in the family, divorce, employment setback, or severe illness can cause somebody who has been moderate, hard working, slim and sober for half a century to find solace in a maze of prescription medicine, shopping, sex, or eating disorders. These are human vices that can sneak up on you when you least expect it.

Fame, talent, and success offer no safety zone. You need only pick up a magazine, newspaper, or search the Internet to find obvious examples. Amy Winehouse, Michael Jackson, Heath Ledger, Brittany Murphy, and Corey Haim all died of overdoses. Tiger Woods, Elliot Spitzer, and former President Clinton tainted their legacies with serial infidelities. The devout Catholic politician and *The Book of Virtues* author Bill Bennett lost $8,000,000 gambling. Radio pundit Rush Limbaugh relied on illegally obtained painkillers after experiencing medical problems. Lindsay Lohan is in and out of court and rehab daily. Actress Winona Ryder was arrested for shoplifting, with antianxiety pills found in her pocket. Comedian Kirstie Alley gained 100 pounds, which she said stemmed from the painful breakup of a relationship. After years of acclaim or clean living or both, these people in the spotlight seemed not to have been aware of their human limitations and frailties.

That anybody can become an addict, and that addicts can lose jobs, fortunes, and relationships does not surprise me in the least. I have seen firsthand that the insidious, not widely publicized effects of addiction are just as bad, if not worse, as the more obvious problems they are widely known to cause. Whether the habit involves food, cigarettes, drugs, liquor, porn, or obsessive gum chewing, I almost always find an unmistakable link between a patient's substance use and the failure to realize his or her dreams.

Happily the reverse of this formula is often true as well. Kicking a compulsion can lead you directly to getting what you want most, whether that is career satisfaction, financial success, better health and appearance, a happy marriage, or deeper relationships with your friends, parents, and children. Keep in mind, however, that severing a dependency on a substance will not happen alone or overnight. It can be a long process, especially if it has been a long-term habit. In fact, it is often the most painful, harrowing, and frightening transformative experience a person will ever go through in his or her entire life. Stopping can also be the most significant emotional decision you will ever make.

When someone realizes they are in the grip of an addiction and need help stopping, there are four main choices available:

1. Quit cold turkey by yourself
2. Check into a hospital or rehabilitation center like The Hazelden or Caron Foundations, Promises, or the Bette Ford Clinic to detox or dry out
3. Start attending twelve-step meetings like Weight Watchers, Alcoholics Anonymous, Gamblers Anonymous, or Overeaters Anonymous
4. Contact a doctor, therapist, or addiction specialist for a one-on-one appointment

In all the studies I have seen, the first choice is the most likely to fail.

That said, no two patients, addictions, or treatments are exactly the same. Many different techniques can be used simultaneously based on an addict's particular needs and personality. For example, one heavy smoker trying to stop will have luck with the nicotine patch. Others trying to get off on nicotine say the patch irritates their skin and gives them bad dreams. In those cases, they might prefer nicotine gum or an inhaler instead. At the same time, it may help this particular smoker to write in his or her journal hourly, avoid all places where people light up, join a gym, and attend weekly Nicotine Anonymous meetings.

It is my belief that you cannot successfully treat an addiction without confronting the deep, emotional issues that are giving rise to the substance abuse in the first place. If you do not dig deeply enough into the roots of the behavior, you will either start using again, or you will switch vices, sometimes without even realizing it.

After my coauthor, Susan, quit her long-term cigarette and marijuana habits, she found herself drinking more. She gave up alcohol only to start chewing sugar-filled gum obsessively, ruining her teeth, and adding too many calories to her diet. When she gave up gum, she started shopping incessantly. Now she jokes that she's become a workaholic addicted to book deals, but it's quite possible she literally is. (What happens if her agent can't sell a new project?

She'll have to deal with the depression underlying this addiction, too.)

Often I warn my patients that I felt like hell for a year after I quit smoking, and they might have to feel like hell for a while, too. The goal is to let yourself feel horrible rather than just switching vices to avoid bad feelings. If your goal is to immediately feel good or happy, the addiction will return. If your goal is living a better, more interesting, and deeper life, sobriety will feel like the right place to live after a while.

A good doctor, addiction specialist, sponsor, AA group, recovery director, or former addict will tell you the truth and be able to guide you out of your addiction. When an addict expects to feel like hell and plans for it in advance, the discomfort will be less scary and more manageable.

If you are serious about quitting, you need to find people in your day-to-day world to help you take responsibility, challenge your assumptions, argue, point out addiction patterns you might not be aware of, while expecting complete honesty and disclosure. I believe that if you are addicted you can learn a lot—and even quit a substance—from reading *Unhooked*. Yet in order to stay unhooked, the book will work best along with finding human beings in your life who you can rely on instead of depending on a substance.

I know how difficult this transition can be. A pack of cigarettes, a bottle of alcohol, or box of cookies is always going to be easier to rely on than a person. The substances are easily available and can be bought, stored, or sometimes even ordered in twenty-four hours a day. Many addicts do not realize how they substitute their addiction for human connection. One patient with a junk food habit slowly became aware that on nights he overate he did not want to have sex—or even snuggle—with his wife. A former smoker noticed that when she quit cigarettes, she would reach for her husband to hug her as a different way to soothe herself.

Stephen, a thirty-six-year-old musician I treated, was drinking, taking painkillers, and snorting heroin. For a loner, new to any kind of therapy and seemingly out of control, he became a very devoted patient. When he was straight, he was brutally honest about his weaknesses and fears. He wanted a connection to somebody badly. I felt close to him, fatherly. He was coming for sessions twice a week for two months, using fewer drugs, making insightful links between his feelings of failure and his need for substances. I was hopeful and believed that he was on his way to healing. Then he disappeared again.

I was worried about him and left messages on his answering machine. He didn't call me back. I wondered what I might be doing wrong and why I couldn't unlock him. Yet intellectually, I knew the drugs were controlling him. Stephen would get stoned and so sucked into his drug world it was all that existed in his life. His therapy, me included, would fall off the radar. I wanted to help him, but the drugs had such a powerful hold on him that I could barely compete. I had seen this before, where a substance replaced all meaningful relationships in a person's life. The substance acted like a jealous and possessive lover, full of false promises such as, "I'll take care of you. Forget everyone else. You only need me." Stephen's addiction had become so intense and omnipresent there was no room at all for closeness with a real person.

It is understandable that an addict in pain or discomfort would reach for a substance to help soothe him- or herself quickly. Why try to get what you need from a person when that is much more complicated and difficult and has so often been disappointing in the past. Unlike a reliable martini, a joint, a cigarette, a pill, a candy bar, Internet porn, or a $400 pair of beautiful designer shoes, people in your world are flawed, flaky, annoying, impossible to control, and often busy with their own lives. They go on vacation, get sick, say stupid things, forget essential facts. Sometimes they even die on you. That does not mean it is better to depend on substances. It means that you have to find human beings who understand what you are going through and want to be relied on, at least for the first year while you are getting clean and sober. These people will be your *core pillars*. The more support you can muster with people whom you can get close to and trust, the more likely you will be successful.

That is not to imply that your core pillars will be perfect. They will not be. They are human and you must allow for their limitations and mistakes. But they must be people whose commitment and reliability will be trustworthy in the end. In order to best assist you, you must be honest with this group of helpers. Do not expect anyone to read your mind. Recovery is an idiosyncratic process and everyone feels and responds differently. It is much easier to be taken care of or helped when you verbalize exactly what will help you. I know that is sometimes hard to determine on your own. One of the benefits of having an addiction therapist or AA or NA sponsor is that he or she will have an overview of your issues and can help you adjust your external reactions, explanations, and requests.

When my coauthor, Susan, was going through a rough nicotine withdrawal, her husband offered to help. He was a nonsmoker who hated her habit and very much wanted her to quit. She was irritable and picked arguments with him when he came home from work at night. These spats often led to screaming matches and tears. I wrote down my prescription: she had to ask him to hold her every night for one hour without talking. No words were said at all. The silence did the trick. Susan felt soothed, her husband felt useful, and they sidestepped the verbal sparring that was hindering their intimacy. It also wound up making them closer and helping her stay smoke-free.

Not every spouse can do this sort of thing so selflessly. Unfortunately some mates make things worse, especially those who are still eating pizza when you are on a diet, or drinking wine when you are struggling in AA. There are no set rules as to who will help and who won't. You might find expensive, well-known, award-winning experts alienating, but feel completely comfortable with former addicts half your age. It is a matter of personal chemistry, trust, and availability. You do not necessarily have to see the people you are relying on every single day or week or month. They can live out of town or out of the country and be connected by daily phone calls, emails, or Skype video chats.

A major step to getting better is to admit that you can't do it alone and to reach out to those who can help you.

CHAPTER 4

HOW TO CULTIVATE CORE PILLARS: ECSTASY, EXTREME SPORTS

Daniel was a patient of mine for five years. A divorced, wealthy businessman of Italian descent in his late fifties who spoke in a detached, matter-of-fact monotone voice, his demeanor and voice came to life—with fear, anxiety, and concern—only when talking about his son, Kevin. Daniel had not been a hands-on dad since he'd left the family when Kevin was twelve. Kevin had grown up and moved to California where he ran into a host of personal problems that included using drugs and alcohol. His father fretted about his son's drug use and self-destructive behavior. Daniel once flew to the West Coast to intervene, afraid Kevin was suicidal. He called me for advice about what to do because he was so frightened. I told him to hospitalize Kevin, which he did, since Kevin sounded so undone.

Daniel's estrangement from his son reminded me of the chasm that had existed between me and my own father, which had intensified after my parents' divorce when I was fourteen. Like Daniel, my dad had offered financial support, but he was too stoic and reserved to connect with me emotionally. I worked hard with Daniel so he could become more expressive of his feelings with his son.

A while after Daniel ended therapy in 2003, he called and left the message: "My son Kevin moved to New York. I'm still worried he's in trouble. Will you see him?" Kevin had been a constant character in his father's therapy; I felt like I already knew him. I told Daniel to give his son my number. Kevin's first message was: "I have more problems than I can say over the phone. My dad insists I meet you." They were both leaving messages mentioning the other one. On one hand, each was reluctant to ask for help for himself directly. On the other hand, it seemed a good sign that they influenced and cared about each other.

While making an appointment with Kevin, I was thinking: *this guy could have a real father for the first time in his life. I could be the bridge reconnecting him and his dad.* I knew that I might be acting out my own dynamics, imposing my paternal fantasy on my patient. Yet my attitude was, "You can do anything as long as it works."

When Kevin came in, he appeared uncomfortable. He said he'd never seen a therapist before. He was twenty-nine, maybe five foot eight, with short hair. He didn't look like Daniel; his olive skin, brown hair, and eyes were darker. He was neatly dressed and in good shape, stocky, rugged in an Outward Bound way. He wore khakis with a polo shirt tucked in and belted. He seemed like a good kid with a good heart. But his eyes gave away his pain. They bored into me, as if desperate to see deeper than the surface. He looked hyper, troubled, haunted. His father had given me an accurate picture.

"Why is your dad so worried about you?" I asked.

"I get so depressed and on edge I can barely function," Kevin said. "I'm much too intense. I live life too hard."

When I asked questions, he admitted he drank beer and smoked marijuana every night, as well as snorting cocaine by himself all weekend, every weekend. That changed when his favorite high became ecstasy. Kevin took ecstasy at dance clubs, where he enjoyed the chaos of nightlife. Many saw "X" as a club kid's drug. Psycho-pharmacologists use the term *empathogen* because it stimulates the capacity to empathize with others. Cocaine, pot, and ecstasy can make you feel filled up, uninhibited, less isolated, and more social. But they didn't make Kevin feel hyper. The drugs surprisingly seemed to stabilize Kevin and made him feel normal and alive. It sounded like he was self-medicating to keep his depression at bay, the way an IV would slowly drip medication into your veins.

Kevin couldn't find meaningful work on the West Coast. He supported himself with help from his dad and by freelancing as a personal trainer. Along with drugs, he was addicted to extreme sports: he'd go bike and ski racing and rock climbing without the right equipment, in places and conditions that presented the highest possible risk. He'd bungee jump, parachute out of planes, and illegally scale tall buildings. He played competitive sports roughly, in radical ways, flirting with physical danger. He liked the thrill, the line between life and death, living on the edge. After he detailed his drug use and obsession with taking risks, I was surprised he was still alive.

I know personally from skiing in high-risk areas and white-water rafting that to survive, you can focus on one thing and one thing only—what you are doing to keep alive. Often with imminent physical danger, awareness of everything else goes away. All emptiness and anxieties vanish when you are so preoccupied, which is one reason addicts are drawn to dangerous activities. While I occasionally ski down difficult slopes or raft on turbulent waters, I learn the rules from more experienced sportsmen who help me master one skill at a time. Kevin, conversely, enjoyed illegal and perilous activities like scaling high buildings, and he made up his own rules. He had a pattern of risky behavior, not paying attention to rules, and going it alone, chasing only the moments of exhilaration. In the throes of an extreme sport, he said, his sadness and all other difficult feelings disappeared.

When Kevin told me he hated school because he couldn't sit still, I suspected attention deficient disorder (ADD) and referred him to Dr. Sands, a psychopharmacologist colleague. I send 20 percent of my patients to medical doctors for such physical ailments as ongoing back spasms, migraine headaches, dizziness, sleeplessness, vision problems, and chronic pain. I also recommend seeing a doctor for psychological extremes such as crippling anxiety or depression, OCD symptoms like excessive hair pulling, and bipolar illness. Sometimes the right medicine makes recovery in psychotherapy possible, even the over-the-counter drugs Aleve or Ibuprofen. Prescriptions to popular (and nonaddictive) antidepressants like Prozac, Paxil, Zoloft, and Wellbutrin can ease the terrible agony to which addicts can be susceptible.

Dr. Sands confirmed that Kevin had ADD. After assurances that Kevin had stopped using cocaine, he prescribed Ritalin, a stimulant referred to as methylphenidate. Although Ritalin acts like speed for people who don't have ADD, patients with attention deficiency feel enormously chilled out and focused on this medication. For Kevin, Ritalin had an immediate, dramatic, and positive effect. "For the first time in my life I feel a sense of calm," Kevin said after taking it the first week.

Once he was more physically calm, Kevin revealed how he felt growing up in a repressed home on the East Coast. His mother was unhappy, ineffectual, did not work or have much of a life on her own. Her parents had died when she was young, and she'd grown up in a sterile orphanage. As a maternal figure, she was not a feeder, a hugger, or encouraging to her kids. Her son called her "cold and empty, with no joy or happiness to give." She was financially dependent on her ex-husband. He had remarried, but she had not. Kevin was not close to his sister or mother and still resented his father. Not only because his dad had walked out on them, but also because he had been a workaholic and emotionally absent during Kevin's childhood.

Daniel felt that his ongoing financial assistance proved he loved his son. But Kevin saw his father as cold, unresponsive, and uncaring, sending checks instead of really being there. He'd left the family when Kevin was twelve, a difficult age for a boy to lose his father, exacerbating a lonely adolescence.

I related to Kevin's story, knowing what it was like to not have a father around at that age to protect you and give you advice, to feel rudderless. When my parents split up, my three siblings and I were shuttled around, living with my mother for three months, then spending the next three months with my father. This went on until I went to boarding school. It was a horrible plan to make us move back and forth, designed for my parents' convenience but not with our welfare in mind. I felt like I never had a home.

I didn't want my son, Jake, to feel like that. When my first wife and I divorced, Jake was seven. Although we'd lived on Long Island, she felt isolated there and was happier near her family on the West Coast. So I allowed them to move there, but I made sure I spoke to Jake on the phone every other day and flew out once a month to be with him. We'd stay at the same Santa Monica hotel for the weekend, going to films and out to eat together; just burgers, nothing fancy. I advise divorced parents who are not custodial not to worry about planning something special during visits with their children. If you ask a kid what their favorite time with their mom or dad is, they'll say, "When we did nothing, when we were just hanging out."

In therapy, Kevin shared more about how lost, lonely, and abandoned he'd felt by his parents. A guy with a normally tough facade, he cried several times, which let me know he felt safe with me. He liked that I respected him, listened, and gave careful advice. He told me I was the closest he'd ever felt to a man. I often thought an important part of my job was playing the role of a good father, the kind I wished I'd had myself. In this case, I did feel very fatherly towards Kevin. Willing to be his "core pillar," I let him lean on me, though unlike other patients, he never called or emailed in between sessions.

I told Kevin it scared and upset me when he risked killing himself. I was less worried when he went to bars with friends after work than when he took drugs on his own. Hidden habits are always more insidious, courting lies, shame, and secrecy. Being alone and keeping it underground is always worse for addicts. Getting the details in the open by talking about their substance use with a therapist, counselor, or AA colleagues is a significant step to recovery. "Lead the least secretive life you can," is my mantra.

In the beginning, the daily Ritalin made Kevin very tired, confirming he had ADD. (Ritalin and Adderall speed up people who don't have ADD.) Kevin took a job at an executive temp agency in New York and now had energy only to work and sleep. I asked him to keep a journal to write down every substance he took and what he felt before, during, and afterwards. He'd never talked about or written down his emotions before. He had never paused long enough in his frantic life for introspection. It was eye opening for Kevin to discover his inner world and how closely his desire to drink, do drugs, and take risks were linked to his emotional ups and downs. He had been involved in many short-term relationships with women but had never let himself get too close. His big discovery was how lonely he'd felt his whole life and how much he craved intimacy.

After he was off cocaine, and cutting down on the pot, beer, and intense sports, I asked, "How long can you go without ecstasy?" I phrased it as a question, not an order, not wanting to alienate him or come off too strong, like a scolding parent.

At one point when he was in college, my son Jake got involved with drugs and alcohol. I admit I did not handle it well. I acted too emotionally. Angrily, I flew to his college, threatening to report him to the dean of his school, and to cut him off financially. I later realized the threat to withhold all financial help was too extreme—Jake needed to feel safe and secure that he had a roof over his head no matter what. I apologized for going too far. Jake wound up quitting the bad habits and forgiving me my overreaction.

When it came to my patients, I could be more clear headed and composed. I did not yet even suggest to Kevin that he should quit marijuana or beer, knowing one can't take away too many bad habits too quickly or at one time. Removing too many support systems simultaneously could cause a relapse or adverse reaction. When Kevin said he was ready to give up ecstasy, I asked, "Are you ready to go through hell?" I wanted to prepare him. He was the competitive sort, so he liked the implicit challenge. He stopped using ecstasy for three days, then for a week. As usual when an addict stops using, difficult feelings surfaced. All emotions were magnified.

Indeed, without drugs, despair washed over Kevin. "I feel like life is pointless. There's no reason to go on," he said, delving into the loneliness, pain, and anxiety that led him to use in the first place. While seeing me twice a week and journaling, he tried Narcotics Anonymous meetings twice weekly. "It makes me feel much less alone," he reported.

Kevin soon stopped ecstasy, cut down on marijuana, and quit extreme sports altogether. He missed the thrill, which took him out of his psyche. He channeled his intense energy into his business. Abstaining from perilous sports activity was a blessing in terms of his physical safety and survival. I was glad he wouldn't fall off a mountaintop or mangle his body around a tree. In some ways I felt he was making a decision to live.

As Kevin drank and toked less, he started going to the gym. I encouraged weight lifting in moderation. It provided a physical release with no peril. Since it was not dangerous, it bored him. When a substance is replaced with something healthier, it never initially feels as good as the original habit. Yet, after three months at the gym, Kevin met someone there. "I felt a connection with this girl, Denise. She's very pretty," he told me. He was thirty-four now, she was twenty-nine.

An addiction not only makes bad things happen, but it keeps goods things from occurring, too. Here's an example of how giving up addictions opens someone up to better experiences that would not have otherwise happened. After they began dating, Kevin asked to bring Denise to therapy. He seemed to want my approval, like bringing a girl home to meet his parents. I already knew his father, now I would be seeing his girlfriend, too.

While getting my graduate degree at the Derner Institute, my mentor Dr. Marks, a psychoanalyst, constantly went against conventional psychoanalytic procedures and folklore. He cared much more about people than ideology. He didn't think it was wrong for a therapist to answer a patient's personal questions, for example, or to accept presents from them, or to bring outside people into therapy sessions. He was open, interested, curious, and even fascinated by whatever was brought to his office—whether it was thoughts, feelings, memories, gifts, friends, lovers, babies, pets, bicycles, or relatives. He assigned the same status to all of them. They all counted as potentially important material. If a patient showed up to see him with a friend and said, "I want him to come sit with me," most therapists would say, "You can't bring him in here." It would be condemned as "acting out" and, as such, deemed unacceptable. Dr. Marks thought that would be the equivalent of saying, "You can't bring in those feelings." I agreed with him, especially when outside intervention involving people who wanted to be proactive increased the chances that my patient could get and stay sober.

I was pleasantly surprised to find Kevin's girlfriend, Denise, to be charming, athletic, hard working, and not into drugs—essential if she was going to be a core pillar. She had a responsible job as an executive in the fashion business. This gave me hope that she'd steer him in a good direction.

As I watched them together, she seemed attentive and devoted. She looked at him a lot, her gaze filled with affection. He seemed calmer next to her, happier, like he felt understood. And safe. They sat close but didn't touch. They appeared connected in a secure way. I never trust a couple who are too touchy feely in front of me, sitting on top of each other. That shows they aren't letting in any space for trouble or ambivalence, and they are only making room for what is wonderful, which is unrealistic.

"I know Kevin did a lot of drugs," Denise said. "I know how anxious and upset he can be. That's why I'm here. When he gets depressed, I want to know how I can help."

"Here's what you can do," I told her. "Show him that you empathize. Describe back to him what he's going through. Say 'I know you feel that there's no point in going on right now. But this will pass.' Listen, but make no judgments. Embrace and accept his dark side. You can't fix him. It's not your job. Let him be depressed but not alone."

At his next individual session, Kevin asked what I thought of Denise. Since I was his surrogate-father figure, he wanted my approval. "You two looked great to me," I said enthusiastically. "She's obviously a substantial woman. It's clear she cares a lot about you. This is your chance for a true emotional bond."

He was intrigued by my reaction, though anxious. I thought the best sign was that Kevin was eager to please Denise and make her happy. I like to see that in a male patient. It's rare when a man can put his woman's happiness before his own (which, according to my theory, eventually leads to his own happiness in turn).

Kevin was off everything but the Ritalin, beer, and pot, which he still smoked occasionally. Some claim marijuana isn't addictive. Hogwash! In some cases it can be extremely addictive. I have seen many patients who could not begin a day, or fall asleep at night, without smoking a joint. You can get hooked on anything used to change how you feel, especially when you're feeling as tortured as Kevin was.

Within the next year, Kevin completely quit drinking and toking. He and Denise moved in together. Although some users find pot makes them paranoid, for Kevin it did a good job of getting rid of his anxiety and depression. Luckily Denise had a sweet, calming effect on him, taking the role the pot once did. I like to think she replaced the drugs in a healthy way. Codependent relationships seem to me selfish, clingy, and obsessive. But good, selfless love has excellent medicinal effects.

Since Kevin was still disconnected from his father, I asked his permission to get Daniel back to therapy. "Yeah, fine, meet with him," Kevin said, apathetically. He had little hope his father would change. I wanted to see if Daniel was willing to learn how to be a good dad and to reconstruct his relationship with his son. I quoted George Eliot: "It is never too late to become what you might have been." You can't change the past, but one can always become a better parent to one's child, no matter how chronologically old or adult that child is. Daniel was definitely interested. I warned him that Kevin needed to express old anger and that he should listen and not be defensive.

The two of them came to six therapy sessions together. They looked uncomfortable and sat far apart; they didn't even know how to be in the same room together. There was no arguing or yelling, but Kevin admitted he felt as much rage towards his dad as love.

"Anything I can to do to help, I will," Daniel promised.

"I know you try and mean well. But there's nothing you can do," Kevin said.

But I didn't believe it was that hopeless. So afterwards, I gave them a homework assignment. I wanted Daniel to take his son out for a meal, just the two of them, at a restaurant in the city. Kevin was reluctant. "We'll have nothing to talk about. We'll just wind up staring at each other," he fretted. Kevin felt like an orphan. His expectations for getting his dad's love were very low.

I persisted, insisting that breaking bread together could be a way to reconnect. I hoped Daniel would step up and be the core pillar that Kevin had always needed. Kevin agreed to give it a try. At dinner, Kevin asked for work advice from his father, who was all too thrilled to share his business wisdom. Kevin was surprised at how much he enjoyed having his father's one-on-one attention. "I can't believe I'm saying this, but I actually had a good time with him," he told me later.

I told Daniel, "Your son needs to know that you love him. Spend more time together. Show interest in his life. Take him to dinner again."

"Look, I'm more than happy to do it. But what should we talk about?" Daniel asked.

"Ask him about his life and work."

"But it'll be like I'm interviewing him."

"Go ahead and interview him. That will show you're interested. Ask him questions."

"He's still angry from his childhood and the divorce," Daniel said. "I can't fix that."

I relayed Maya Angelou's idea that "you did then what you knew how to do, and when you knew better, you did better."

They went out to dinner once a week, choosing steak houses, small French bistros, Italian cafés, sometimes burger joints. It was never about the food. It was about the company and Kevin finally being fed by his dad. At these meals, Daniel always paid the bill. He was happy to feed his son, literally and metaphorically. He was so proud of Kevin, he was glowing. Daniel once took Kevin and Denise to dinner together, but I suggested he go back to seeing his son once a week alone.

On September 11, 2001, Kevin was working on Wall Street and witnessed the attacks on the World Trade Center. Like many New Yorkers, it agitated and upset him for several months. I was living in Battery Park City with my second wife and young daughter, close to Ground Zero. My family was also severely traumatized by getting caught in the middle of the disaster. One winter day during a session with Kevin, my wife called on my emergency cell phone, which I always picked up. There had been an explosion at a Con Ed plant. Still frightened by her experiences a few months earlier, she feared it was another terrorist attack. I apologized for the interruption, then told Kevin that my wife and daughter had been hurt on 9/11, and now my wife was afraid it was happening all over again. As somebody who had lived through it himself, Kevin grasped the situation immediately and said, "You gotta go. Get out of here." I felt like we were comrades fighting the same war.

When Kevin decided he wanted to stop therapy and "move on," I wondered if by sharing my angst about 9/11, I had become more agitating than healing. Kevin's father had been out of state at the time and provided the kind of relief and perspective I could not. Regardless, Kevin and I agreed that he did not need me in the same way after he got his real dad back.

Kevin fully overcame his addictions to cocaine, ecstasy, marijuana, and extreme sports by depending on me, colleagues from Narcotics

Anonymous, the love of his girlfriend, and a weekly dinner with his dad. To the best of my knowledge the two men are still dining together weekly.

Since the memories of the World Trade Center attacks haunted my family relentlessly, we decided to move to Arkansas, where my wife is from, which felt safer. My son Jake has now graduated from law school in New York. When I come to town every six weeks, we always have a meal together. A few times he's brought his girlfriend, which is nice. But I let him know my priority is being alone with him so we can catch up one-on-one. I wouldn't dream of flying East without taking my son out to dinner.

WHERE TO TURN FOR HELP TODAY

Unfortunately not all addicts will be lucky enough to have a concerned mate and willing parent at their side to aid in their addiction battle. Still, recovery meetings and addiction specialists are readily available and offer a great place to start building a foundation of core pillars. There are often many nurturing human beings you can find to help and support you. By proving you are capable of change, those who have disappointed you in the past might step up and change, too. Sobriety brings lots of surprises. Sometimes the people who wind up being able to help you most are the ones who have been standing in front of you all along.

Here is a list of people you might want to consider confiding in and depending on.

1. Sponsors or fellow quitters from Alcoholics Anonymous, Narcotics Anonymous, Overeaters Anonymous, Weight Watchers, SmokeEnders, or American Cancer Society group leaders or fellow members. The benefits of finding allies in these organizations are that they have like-minded goals, are often free of charge or cost very little, have meetings every day and night in most cities, and are available twenty-four hours a day.

2. An addiction specialist, psychologist or social worker. It would be optimum to find an expert in the field whom you like and trust and to commit to one or two session a week for at least a year. If you can't afford it, ask your therapist if he or she might be willing to work on a sliding scale or offers group therapy, which is often a much less-expensive option.

   Check to see what is covered by your health insurance. My coauthor, Susan, didn't realize her insurance provided fifty sessions a year of addiction therapy costing her only a $25 copay.

3. Drug counselors, doctors, psychopharmacologists, and pharmacists who might provide you with facts, tests, prescriptions for medications and the latest weapons in fighting addiction. For example, the professionals you consult will be aware that the nicotine nasal spray or the antidepressant, Zyban, have helped many smokers to quit, and that the New York State Health Department is currently giving out nicotine patches for free.

4. Other experts in health professions including nutritionists, personal trainers, exercise teachers, acupuncturists, massage therapists, martial arts teachers, or yoga instructors whose goals are healthy and align with yours.

5. Workout buddies or teammates in a club or group sport you enjoy.

6. Work partners, agents, managers, editors, bosses, bodyguards, personal assistants, and colleagues who have gone through similar problems and are invested in your recovery.

7. Close friends with whom you're comfortable and who've overcome similar addictions or problems.

8. Mates, parents, or children who don't have the same addiction you have and want to help.

9. An uncle, aunt, cousin, niece, nephew, or another relative who either has had similar problems or is clean and willing to listen.

10. Online addiction groups, websites, or chat rooms can offer round-the-clock support and share new information. See if

they can help you locate real (and not only virtual) colleagues in your area who could become the core pillars you need to lean on. What matters most is finding people who can really understand your struggle and the seriousness of your mission to lead a cleaner, better, more honest life.

CHAPTER 5

FEELINGS MISINFORM: COCAINE, SEX & SHOPPING

"I feel like I'm ugly and stupid and won't ever find anyone to love me," my patient, Courtney, once told me.

While I advocate the poet W. H. Auden's proclamation that you should "believe your pain," I also tell my patients that feelings misinform. Feelings, it must always be remembered, are not facts. It is not unusual for an addict to mistake his or her thoughts, fears, and emotions for reality and the truth. I feel this, so it must be true. I think this, so it is, therefore, fact. With many habitual substance abusers, wires were crossed at an early age, parents and other caretakers were not dependable, and internal voices were unreliable. Feelings replaced rational thought and took on a huge and compelling life of their own.

The primary goal of good parenting should be to make your offspring feel safe. When that doesn't happen, a child might grow up believing that the world is a dangerous place and that people are out to get them. Those leftover feelings from the past often have no roots in the actual world. Many addicts I've seen were disappointed by adults early on and thus had no confidence that they were being protected. Since their own internal voices failed to reassure them or make them feel secure, they turned to substances to manage bad feelings. When that happens, the downside is that internal resources all ground to a halt. The upside is that addictions actually do a great job of quieting turbulent feelings when nobody else is there to help, at least temporarily. That was the case with Courtney.

When she initially left me a phone message, Courtney sounded smart, engaging, and well spoken. I wondered if she was lying to herself, or to me, or both. I had already been warned by the West Coast colleague who had referred her that Courtney was "really into cocaine, a complete mess." At the Long Island substance abuse clinic where I had been working, I had learned early on that external appearances proved nothing; the best dressed person could be the worst addict. Courtney sounded enthusiastic about seeing me. She was the first patient to call after I opened up my private practice in Manhattan in May 1983, so I was eager to see her, too.

Early the next day she came to the small office I had just rented on 19th Street and 5th Avenue. She was a twenty-two-year-old Protestant college graduate from Gramercy Park. She was five foot seven and dressed in a beige silk blouse and nice jeans; she looked to be a mix of an all-American girl and a hippie. She had a big smile and long, wild, curly light blonde hair all the way down her back. Nobody would have guessed she was a drug-addicted mess.

Often with patients, amid the cacophony of things going on during a session—appearance, subject matter, words, tone, and feelings— there is one characteristic that relays what is really going on more clearly than anything else. With Courtney, her naturally curly, chaotic blonde hair seemed to most accurately reveal her internal disarray.

In our first meeting, Courtney answered my questions rapidly, a long story spilling out of her with no time sequence, no internal theme, a kind of chaotic rambling that seemed driven by extreme anxiety. She chronicled her wealthy, society-page family's private schools, servants, and trust funds. Her mother had died when she was six. Her father had a dental degree but was more often playing tennis and bridge at his country club than working. He had many girlfriends in the years since her mother had died, but he had never remarried. Her older brother was a pharmacist. He had gone away to a prep school, as had Courtney. She had recently earned her bachelor's degree from Reed College. In twenty minutes of her nonstop monologue, she had not said one word about her drug use.

"What about the supposed coke problem I've been told you have?" I asked, wanting her to know what I already knew.

She seemed unfazed by my statement and admitted that her drug use started when she was a teenager. But her real problem, Courtney insisted, was that her mother had died of a drug overdose of barbiturates and pain medications. She spilled layers of complex family issues. Both of her parents had many affairs that their children knew about from an early age. They had abused alcohol as well as drugs—uppers, downers, speed, painkillers. As a dentist, her father had easy access to drugs.

Courtney's mother had used her to fill illegal prescriptions that she had forged on Courtney's father's prescription pads. As a little girl, Courtney remembered going to the local pharmacy and innocently asking, "Would you fill this for my mommy?" Bringing home the pills, her mother would ingest them in front of her. By the time she was five years old, Courtney was begging her mother not to take them, pleading, "But mommy, they're not good. You know what they do to you."

I identified with Courtney's feelings of confusion and neglect, knowing what it felt like growing up lost in a wealthy WASPy Manhattan family. I hoped the overlap might help. I could see her world from the inside out better than she could. I was thirty years old at the time, eight years older than Courtney, married, and living on Long Island. I had recently finished my doctoral degree and had been licensed in clinical psychology in New York State. Courtney was single and now living on the Upper West Side, but the parallels of our lives were striking. She had gone to Dalton, an elite and expensive private school. My mother and sister had gone to a Dalton-like school. I had dated Dalton girls. Well, I would have dated Dalton girls if I'd had the courage to ask any of them out back then. Courtney's mother was popping pills, my mother was drinking, and drinking hard.

Courtney recalled the day her elementary school teacher told her she had to go home in the middle of the afternoon. A black limousine was waiting outside. "I knew that one of my parents was dead," she said. "I believed in that moment that I could choose which parent had died. I thought, which one of them do I want to be dead? It was crazy. But I chose my father." She decided she had to make a decision, like *Sophie's Choice*, in her own mind. But she was wrong. Her mother had died of an overdose.

"I used to think that I could control what happened if only I'd do the right thing," she told me. "One day I was walking along the street and I suddenly thought if I grabbed that bird with my bare hands and ate it, I could bring my mother back." Courtney was constantly haunted by such thoughts, accompanied by extreme anxiety, despair, and anguish.

She was highly superstitious and believed her thoughts were so powerful they could control the universe. They could even determine who lived and died. This could be mistaken for bipolar illness or OCD, but in Courtney's case it wasn't. Since many addicts mistake random thoughts and feelings for the truth, I explained to Courtney that just because she felt fragile, as if she would fall apart at any second, this did not mean that she would actually fall apart in reality. It meant only that she would *feel* like she was going to fall apart. It was important to understand the difference.

Although her mother had serious substance problems, Courtney deeply identified with her and believed her mother had loved her. Her attachment to her mother was stronger than to her father, who was an absent parent. There was no physical or sexual abuse in the family, but there were no rules or regulations either. Courtney lived off a trust fund. She admitted that she had easily spent $10,000 that semester alone on cocaine. When she called her father to ask for another $10,000, he asked, "For what?"

"I need new clothes," she lied.

"Good for you for dressing well," he said, issuing another check. No rules applied.

I had never treated someone addicted to both sniffing and shooting up cocaine. Courtney had been doing this for three years. To my surprise, she said that doing drugs was never fun for her. She was not a casual user seeking the drug for pleasure. She was an addict from day one. She had hated the effect that it had on her, but she could not stop. Why did she keep using if it didn't bring her happiness or a thrill? Because using took all her painful thoughts and feelings away and replaced them with a tense, jumpy, jaw-clenching focus. She used drugs to externalize the intense anxiety she was feeling inside. However unpleasant it was, it worked. She erased internal pain, replacing it with an external anxiety, which she found easier to cope.

This is often the case with addicts, and it is a strong argument that substance abusers are certainly not pleasure-seeking hedonists. Often addictions bring no joy or amusement to the user whatsoever. Instead, they take away intolerable pain, depression, and anxiety, and replace it with a numbness, or uneasy equilibrium that make mere survival seem possible. Substances often function as self-medication for an addict's usually undiagnosed distress.

For an addict, all excitement is suspect. A gleeful, high, soaring feeling that helps you escape your day-to-day existence often causes you to make stupid decisions. A gambler in the heat of a poker game bets next month's rent because Lady Luck is about to smile on him or her. A drunk at a bar gets behind the wheel of a car or goes home with a stranger, denying there is any danger. A shopaholic buys an expensive living room set, convinced that new furniture will save his marriage or change her social standing. Because the unconscious aim of addictive behavior is to alter, cure, or escape one's emotions, addictions inspire, fuel, and enhance these kinds of self-deceptions.

Courtney confessed she was sleeping with many different men. Her sexual activity was irrational, reckless, drug induced. It was motivated by all kinds of misconceptions and a lack of any sense of what she herself felt or believed. She thought if she kissed a guy and led him on, she would have to sleep with him, even though she did not like sex. She could not say no or take a stand. She could not question this or other irrational systems that dictated what she could or could not do.

One time as a teenager she stayed out all night and her dad found out that she had been with a boy. The next day, as punishment, he made her watch several tennis matches with him. Was he punishing her, or rewarding her, by finally giving Courtney his attention for three hours straight? It did not make sense to her. She had no self-esteem, no self-regulation, no blueprint. All the rules about relationships were made up in her head because her parents were never role models and never provided any useful or rational road map to follow. Her life seemed dangerously out of control.

At this point, working in my Long Island clinic, the substance abusers I treated were mostly adolescent patients between the ages of fourteen and eighteen. They used alcohol, marijuana, and cocaine for short periods of time. Parents, schools, and courts often mandated treatment. With these kids, their drug use tended to represent more of a rebellious acting out—not atypical of teenagers. Listening to Courtney's sex and cocaine litany was different. It was a dramatic introduction to how chaotic every area of an adult addict's life and psyche could be.

Toward the end of my very first session with Courtney, she said, "I'm going to Greece for three months. I can see you when I get home."

"Greece? For what?" I asked.

"Summer vacation," she'd answered.

"With who?"

"Alone," she said. "I'll be back the middle of August."

It seemed odd that a twenty-two-year-old girl who could barely take care of herself was traveling to a foreign country alone for three months. Yet, as a clinical psychologist, I had been trained to follow the patient's lead, to be a neutral figure, not to get too emotionally involved, not interject a strong opinion. I said, "Okay," and we made an appointment for after she returned in late August. I did not think twice about Courtney's trip until weeks later when I was talking to my mentor, Dr. Brian Marks.

I had first met Dr. Marks in 1977 when I enrolled in his course on Sigmund Freud. He was a short, stocky, funny, impulsive, provocative, Jewish maverick. He smoked heavily (I was smoking too at the time). Before he became a therapist he had been a guitarist in a rock band. He was a renegade with a distinctive wild side. I loved him immediately. After class one day, I handed him my fifty-page paper about Freud and anthropology, suggesting that the way he had organized his course was just like the way I had organized my essay. He thought that was ludicrously arrogant of me. He hated unearned arrogance and felt that he had worked hard for the admiration he garnered, whereas I had not. He was right. Still, I was bored by my overly academic professors and wanted him as my supervisor. I later told him so when I ran into him in the men's room. He said, "I used to hate you because you were arrogant and insulting. But now I love you and I'll supervise you whenever you want."

I adopted him as my substitute father. A friend joked that our connection was like Freud and Jung, but I was too emotionally involved to see it. I discussed all of my patients with him and told him about Courtney and her trip to Greece. He was surprised and said, "Why did you let her go?" What a question! Here was a noted professor of psychology, the head of my doctoral program, and my boss at the substance abuse clinic asking why I had not boldly interjected myself into this adult person's life during her very first session. Once in a while Dr. Marks would say a sentence or ask me something in a certain tone of voice that would forever change my way of thinking. This was one of those moments. The minute he asked why I had let this out-of-control patient go abroad by herself for so long, I saw that I had made a mistake; I should have at least tried to stop Courtney from going. Dr. Marks's blunt question gave me permission to let myself know what I knew, that it was crazy for someone so unstable to go away by herself. I had formed a strong opinion about her trip to Greece when she originally said it, but I had repressed it. Dr.

Marks was teaching me to have the hands-on, direct approach that eventually came to characterize my addiction therapy.

"How could you ever have let me to go to Greece in the condition I was in?" Courtney later asked me. My style had changed so much over the next few years that it no longer made sense to her that I had been so passive in the face of her thoughtless plan. During the years Courtney was in treatment with me, she had become a drug-abuse counselor. At a certain juncture in her own counseling practice, she began to refer difficult addicts to me. She knew how forceful I now allowed myself to be and how my opinionated approach tended to get better results with addicts than more nonaggressive therapies.

But when I first met her in 1983, I was younger and more reserved when it came to early interventions, less willing to share my opinions and personal story with those I was treating. I was reluctant to get into trouble by challenging conventional ways of working. I was more inclined to follow the rules I was taught, even when my patients did not seem to benefit from my detached, noninterventionist position. Years later, I admitted to Courtney it was a mistake that I hadn't tried to stop her from going abroad and apologized.

I was just figuring out that effective addiction therapy had to be different from the slower, analytic methods used to treat general neurosis and depression. Calm, cerebral questioning or "free association" with a therapist who was a blank screen was simply ineffective in the face of extreme, dangerous substance abuse that required more intensity and faster intervention. Treating addicts required a different focus and skill set than I was taught in training. Patients were not coming to me for academic theory or even to deepen their understanding of themselves. They were people who were very depressed, in pain, out of control, hurting themselves daily, and begging for assistance.

Courtney gave an alcoholic friend of hers my number and he came in for a session. While this young man had been studying at an Ivy League college, he had been in psychoanalysis four times a week. In his first session with me, he said, "I learned all about my past, where my problems had come from, and it was great. I would leave the sessions, go to a bar, and really think deeply about all those insights while I got completely plastered."

One reason that twelve-step methods work so well with addicts is that as a group they do not need to spend a hundred hours reviewing or being questioned about their horrible childhoods. They need to be told to stop right now or they might die. (Once they are clean, they can then go back, unravel, and better understand their horrible childhoods.) It is why twelve-step programs do so well to stop addictions. Many therapists are taught to focus on the past, be unobtrusive, collect tons of data, and to provide insight into how current behavior is rooted in childhood. Leaders of AA and similar programs realize that knowledge does not help addicts get clean. Taking action is essential to the solution. Insight alone never helped anyone quit anything. Stopping drinking is what stops you from drinking.

Yet some people are not comfortable in group settings and many, like Courtney, thrive with one-on-one attention and personalized strategies. Every case is different, but I learned that if I did not intervene fast and forcefully enough, patients would often not return for a second session and go on to ruin themselves or people around them. The process of buying drugs in bad neighborhoods itself could be very dangerous, especially for a young woman on her own. The narcotics sold could be laced with poison. While stoned on substances, patients picked up strangers in bars and brought them home. Their sense of judgment was screwed up, so they might drive high or, like Courtney's mother, take drugs in front of their children.

I also saw how quickly addicts gave up on therapy. Very often, after just one unenlightened session, they would throw in the towel. Thus, the window of opportunity was small. Most addicts expected to be disappointed. They did not believe anyone could help them. Only their substance could help. At the same time, they were often out of control and desperately wanted limits to be set. That was why they were coming to see me. But sometimes they hoped I would fail so they could justify their substance use. As my practice thrived, I allowed myself to become more bold, direct, and confrontational. I wanted to make an immediate impression that grabbed the addicts so they would commit to therapy and getting clean.

When Courtney returned from her trip abroad, I was relieved to hear that she had not used any cocaine in Greece. In a dramatic change of circumstances or setting, many substance abusers suddenly stopped using because all of their psychic space was filled up with the excitement of a new experience. The associations having to do with the substance use were gone. This told me that Courtney was capable of stopping. She had not yet been able to "score any" since she'd returned to New York. I felt that if she went back to using the drug, her life would not move forward. I wanted to fill the space previously occupied by the white powder. Since she could afford it, and needed it, she started seeing me four times a week. I realized that in order to get clean Courtney might initially be able to replace her dependency on reckless sex and drugs to being dependent on therapy instead.

In our tenth session I told her, "You need to stop having casual sex altogether. It is much too dangerous. You do not even like it. You do it because you are terrified of being alone. You are clinging to anyone who will lie in your bed and hold you." She agreed and seemed to follow through with her promise to stop. I saw her promiscuity as a symptom of her confusion and loneliness. Perhaps insisting she stop made her feel less alone and that knowing somebody cared about her and was looking out for her best interest was enough.

A few sessions later, I went on a blunt campaign to get her off drugs. This was the first time I had directly pushed a patient to get off a substance. It was a major turning point in her life and in my career. This approach did not work in many later cases. Yet, since Courtney was so young and bereft of family, I intentionally acted like the omnipotent parent. I wondered if she craved a concerned parent more than the cocaine. It could be that she was just ready to get healthy and to let somebody intervene on her behalf.

Unfortunately, right after she quit cocaine, Courtney started excessively shopping for high-priced clothes at Madison Avenue stores and boutiques. She would come into my office upset that she'd bought a $700 purse, explaining how the salesperson had been so nice that she could not say no, the same way she had not been able to say no to sleeping with a boy who had kissed her.

As much as I did not believe in switching addictions as a cure, there was a hierarchy of habits. Although cocaine, indiscriminate sex, and obsessive credit card use were all ways to get away from difficult feelings, at least she would not die or overdose from too much shopping. But I did point out what she was doing and imposed such rules as "You are not allowed to spend more than $100 on anything without first discussing it in therapy." By slowing down her purchases this way, she was able to get rid of much of the impulsiveness.

Within six months, Courtney stopped drinking, drugs, sleeping with strangers, and spending money indiscriminately. Yet it took her almost three decades to unravel the pain behind her addictions. This is not unusual. I have seen many patients like Courtney who had been addicts since they were in their teens. When they started using substances, their emotional development stopped. When they quit using addictions to cope, they were still teenagers emotionally and had to start over from where they left off.

I still have weekly sessions with Courtney. Twenty-eight years is the longest duration that I have ever treated a patient. Over the years, I have met all the characters in Courtney's psychodramas in my office.

Her widowed father came in for ten sessions, ostensibly to talk about Courtney's problems and how he could help, but I thought he really wanted to talk about himself. He was stiff and unhappy. I told him that he could still help his daughter enormously if he would become a better father now. I suggested he call and see her more often, ask about her work and therapy, make their time together more about her. He told Courtney he liked me. Her father was important to her, so she was pleased. They were able to forge a better bond before he died of pneumonia in 1995. I met her brother, who loved playing tennis like her father. He had his own crisis a few years later and came to see me for ten sessions.

I raised serious questions about Courtney's first husband, but unfortunately she would not bring him into therapy until after she'd married him. He was a grant writer she'd wed at twenty-seven. She had a fantasy that he was this nice, safe guy with a steady job. He seemed passive, a hanger on. He was not a drug addict, but he was later accused of embezzling funds, which shocked both of us. Why had she married him? Because she was afraid to be alone and was still blindly followed her feelings instead of slowing down and learning how to let her brain accurately assess somebody.

At thirty-three Courtney remarried and had a son with her second spouse, someone I'd also tried to get her away from—with no luck. He turned out to be a violent drunk. She divorced him after two years. The closest relationship in her life was with her son from that marriage. In some ways that maternal connection replaced the closeness she had desperately missed from her own mother.

At thirty-five, Courtney finally took my advice to slow down and date the right way, without jumping into bed or moving in together too fast. She was not used to old-fashioned courtships and we discussed how important it was for her to take her time and make better choices. She had her hair cut shorter, dyed, and shaped differently. It was neater, more stylish and tame. While her hair became more conservative, she was more expressive, verbal, emotionally explosive. "Why the hell was the baby crying all night?" she once yelled. Another session she came in fuming, "I'm going to fire that stupid babysitter." Addicts often have a wild side, so actually discovering her natural energy and primal passion was progress.

In the nineties, when Courtney was thirty-nine, she married a successful architect who had a son from a previous union. I found him to be smart, stable, sane, and very grounding for her. In her forties, Courtney had a second child, a daughter. During Courtney's therapy sessions, I challenged her to extend her counseling work and go back to school to become a social worker.

While Courtney was finishing her master's degree, I went through my own career upheaval. When a group of graduate students complained about a course they didn't want to be required to take at Adelphi, I set up a meeting with them and a few professors without consulting my boss, Dr. Marks. He became furious that I waffled in my strict adherence to his procedures. He was right; I had started doing things my own way, alienating committees he deemed important and not being diplomatic. I learned that teaching institutions are complex political systems and that one had to be a careful strategist to rise to the top of. I was not a good team player and thus became a liability for Dr. Marks.

He wound up firing me from my teaching position, throwing me out of his program and his life. He called me into his office and literally said, "You're out, that's final," and then stormed out of his own office, leaving me standing there alone. It was the ultimate rejection for somebody like me who had serious abandonment issues. (I once tried to copy his dramatic exit and left a misbehaving fifteen-year-old patient of mine alone in my office. It completely backfired. She locked me out, taping notes to me behind picture frames that I did not find until years later. They turned out to be notes expressing her hopes for finding love and fame in the future that she was too embarrassed to tell me in person.)

Dr. Marks refused to have any contact with me for five years. His rejection was excruciatingly painful. I loved and admired him so much and saw him as such an exalted mentor/father figure that my rational brain didn't compute that he was a human being with flaws and shortcomings. I realized that my feelings of adoration and need had misinformed me.

Although it was difficult to separate from him, our falling out was ultimately liberating. It allowed me to become more of my own kind of therapist and the head of my own clinic at The Village Institute. I started sending Dr. Marks notes and holiday cards, telling him that his brilliance and inspiration had survived our split. In response, he left a warm message saying that he had been following my career and that he wanted me to be successful and happy. I recently called to refer someone to his private practice. We had a good talk. I was finally able to see him as a three-dimensional person with strengths and weaknesses.

Courtney often talks to me about her successful practice. I wonder if being Dr. Marks' protégé for so long allowed me to be a better mentor to Courtney.

"My life is so good now, but I feel sadder than I ever have," Courtney recently told me, still trying to untangle her chaotic childhood, the cocaine days, and what her mother's death at such an early age meant to her. I think it's major progress that Courtney finally feels safe enough to let herself mourn. As the late British psychoanalyst Wilfred Bion suggested, turbulent feelings are problems to be solved. Courtney's are no longer unbearable monsters she has to run from at all costs.

HOW TO TELL IF YOUR FEELINGS MISINFORM

1. Write down exactly what you are feeling in your journal, even if it seems extreme. If you were fired, this might come out like: "I fear I will never get a job again, I will lose my apartment, and die broke and penniless."

2. Pretend someone you love wrote the above sentence. What would you tell your closest friend, spouse, and child if they said this about themselves?

3. Pretend you are a trial lawyer arguing the opposite point. In this case, maybe you'd list every job you ever had, every time you've ever been fired and recovered.

4. Show your writing to a trusted friend. Listen if he or she has another point of view than what you wrote.

5. If the worst you wrote were to actually come true, what would you do? Make a list of resources you might have in a financial

emergency, like moving back in with a parent or former room-mate, borrowing money from a sibling, or finding a cheaper apartment or less-expensive city.

6. Don't act on your feelings right away. For example, don't call your parents and say, "I think I might need to move back home," yet. Give yourself more time to process your feelings—with a friend or relative you trust, if possible—before doing anything.

7. Do something nice for yourself before reacting. Take a walk, get a manicure or massage, read a book or magazine you like, go to the movies. Calm down. Allow space for thinking. Then reappraise.

8. Make rules about your reaction in this mood. For example, one of my patients must wait at least twelve hours before answering a difficult email.

9. Read what you've written back to yourself a day later and see if your mood has changed the feeling at all or given you any other perspective on it.

10. Share this feeling with a close friend, mate, or relative you trust.

11. Bring this up with your therapist, recovery group, or other core pillars. You might be pleasantly surprised to learn that many people feel this way at times. By that doesn't mean your feeling is true or helpful or that it's not just a fleeting emotion that will dissipate when a cooler head prevails.

CHAPTER 6

UNDERSTANDING HOW ADDICTS THINK: HALLUCINOGENIC DRUGS & STEALING

Doug had a good reason for coming to see me in the fall of 1986: his therapy was mandated by a judge. The sixteen-year-old high school student had been arrested for breaking and entering. His choice was jail or me.

When I was the clinical director of the Baldwin Council Against Drug Abuse, Long Island judges knew we were a free clinic that specialized in substance-abuse treatment. Therefore they routinely sentenced thirteen-to-eighteen-year-old substance abusers, truants, and troublemakers to a year or more of mandatory treatment with us. Whenever I had an exceptionally uncooperative patient, I would say something like, "It's your choice—jail seven days a week or my office once a week. Believe me, my office is a much better place than a prison cell. But if you prefer, I will tell the judge to send you off to jail instead . . ." That usually cut through bad attitudes pretty quickly.

Doug did not have a bad attitude at all. When he walked into my office, he was watchful and respectful. He was wearing baggy jeans, a T-shirt, and sneakers, casual and appropriately sloppy for his age. He was five foot ten, with a medium build and dirty blond hair. His demeanor, choice of wire-rimmed eyeglasses, and the careful way he watched his surroundings gave the impression of a self-conscious, intellectual teenager.

When I asked questions about his background, I learned that Doug was the middle of three children in a liberal Jewish suburban family. His father owned an auto shop. His mother worked full-time at a local mall. The parents sounded busy but clueless. I often found that the parents of a substance abuser had lost touch with their child and had become oblivious to even blatant signs of trouble. Doug's older sister was married and out of the house. His little brother was following in his footsteps, heading toward drugs and truancy. Doug was a straight-A student who barely studied. He skipped school often, but his teachers did not express concern as long as he kept his grades up. That was the kind of education he was getting.

He appeared to be engaged in a great deal of sociopathy, exhibiting behavior that was indifferent to the rules of society. This is common for addicts who tend to feel that their powerful needs trump the rules and regulations followed by other people. Doug was a cunning rule breaker who lived according to his personal agenda. Before getting caught during a recent robbery he'd committed, it seemed he could get away with practically anything. He had little parental supervision from his disorganized family where kids grabbed food on the fly and did drugs when they felt like it. He told me the story of breaking into a house in his neighborhood which led to his arrest and ultimately to his mandated presence in my office.

"Why did you do it?" I wanted to know.

"Because I was hungry," he answered.

I was surprised by his answer. "What does that mean?"

"I hadn't eaten. Really," he said. "I was raiding the refrigerator. And stole jewelry while I was at it."

It turned out that breaking into the house had set off a silent alarm that he did not hear. The police had surprised him when he was sitting at the kitchen table, eating food from the refrigerator. He was not yet in possession of the jewels when the police nabbed him. The home belonged to friends of his parents.

I kept interrogating him. "Was it the first time you've done this?"

"Is this confidential?" he asked. "Or will you tell the judge?"

He was a smart kid; he did not want to incriminate himself for more crimes.

"Here are my rules," I said. "I am in touch with the judge only to tell him when you come to therapy and if you miss a session. The judge will know nothing else. He knows not to even ask me. If the authorities did ask me for more information, I would go to jail myself before answering them." As someone who had so intensely searched for parental attention and guidance my whole life, I intentionally spoke with conviction and authority, once again trying to emulate the tone of a powerful, concerned father.

"Okay," Doug said. "What do you want to know?"

"Tell me about your illegal activities."

He admitted that he was taking LSD, Mescaline, and Psilocybin mushrooms several times a week when he was alone. These were hallucinogenic, escapist drugs that produced a kind of unplugging of consciousness from reality for hours at a time. I suspected Doug wanted to get out of his life, to get away from his hurt.

Doug's pain was on the surface, close to consciousness. He had yet to develop any systems for masking problems more complicated than drugs and theft. He was frustrated with his family and complained about his parents often. His mother sounded like she felt stuck in a miserable marriage. Her husband didn't seem to care about her or pay her much attention. He was not particularly successful. Her biggest enjoyment came from working so, in essence, all of her happiness took place outside the home. They were not bad or abusive people, they were just unhappy and so busy taking care of themselves that they forgot to love their kids.

"Let me tell you a story about my dad," Doug said. "He has a rule that I have to take out the garbage twice a week. When I forgot last week, Dad says, 'Doug, take out the garbage.' I put on my strong voice and said, 'I don't feel like doing it now.' So in a resigned voice he says, 'Okay, I'll dump the garbage,' and goes and does it himself. Isn't that pathetic? Why didn't he haul off and slug me? Cause he's too weak. That's why. That's the best my father's got."

Like most teenage boys, Doug wanted a father who was strong and forceful. They feel deep disappointment with wimpy paternal figures and become disdainful of all adults when their own fathers are ineffectual. I recalled how disappointed I had been that my own dad wasn't a stronger role model who could have taken charge and protected me. It left me feeling the way Doug did, as if I had to take care of myself because there was nobody in the world who had my back. Although I didn't know it at the time, that was probably why by the time I was Doug's age, I was addicted to smoking, reaching for cigarettes to soothe me and shield me from all internal pain.

"Why do you do drugs?" I asked Doug.

"Because I like them." I saw that he did not yet have a clue about his deeper motivations.

He did not like the usual teenage substances of alcohol, pot, and cigarettes, nor was he very interested in sex. He had a difficult time getting close to people. He was stuck in the typical addict's paradox—shunning human dependency while at the same time desperately craving closeness, understanding, and intimacy. While high, Doug would listen to the Grateful Dead or Bob Dylan, wander around the woods by his house, sometimes breaking into his school at night or during weekends. He read novels by Kurt Vonnegut, Aldous Huxley, and—oddly—business books. His drug habit cost him $50 a week. Since his parents gave him a $10 weekly allowance, rather than asking for more, he supplemented this by regularly breaking into local houses. He took jewelry, watches, and other valuables he later sold at local pawn shops to pay his drug dealer.

"So you're a nice, Jewish serial thief who wants to be a CEO?" I asked.

His modus operandi was original, something I had never seen on *Law & Order*. During every single heist, before he was finished vandalizing the house, he would go into the refrigerator, take out food, sit down at the table, and eat a meal. The symbolism here was both fascinatingly complex and self-evident.

"I'm demoting your diagnosis," I told him. "You're not really a thief. You are a little boy who wants to be fed. You have never been fed well at home by your parents, and that is what you are really after. You want to sit at the dinner table with a family and eat a good meal and feel that you are loved and taken care of."

When I said this, Doug looked very sad. Tears welled up in his eyes, as if he had never thought of this before but recognized it as the truth. He was an intriguing case. I had never treated someone addicted to the combination of dropping acid, taking magic mushrooms, stealing, and raiding refrigerators in the houses of strangers. He was acting out his psychological needs in some of the most undisguised ways I had ever seen.

"Listen, I think you are a smart kid and you're going to be a very successful businessman. After all, lots of wealthy business guys are just legal thieves," I joked. "So you're already well on your way."

He smiled, seeming appreciative for being so accurately summed up and understood.

"But you have to do what I tell you."

"What do you want me to do?" he asked.

"Stop doing drugs, which are bullshit. Stop stealing, which will keep you pigeonholed as a petty criminal," I said. "And you need to learn how to cry without shame."

I explained to Doug my theory that if he did not accept his difficult feelings of anger and sadness, he would have to continue taking drugs and stealing. I was sure that if he could cry in front of me, someone who cared about him, he would be able to stop his sociopathic behavior. Ripping off his neighbors' houses seemed a metaphor for taking things that he felt he deserved but was not getting, like food and love. If he could actually experience his deep longings and disappointments, I hoped he would not be so compelled to act out. He agreed that seeing me once a week was better than jail and grew to like seeing me. As far as I know, he never stole anything again. But the drugs were a different story.

Although bright, Doug was too distant and suspicious to allow himself to feel close to me at first. He was earnest, serious, and careful in what he said. (He eventually became much more open and funny.)

But he did share his aspirations right away, which seemed fairly banal to me. He was a materialist who wanted to own many objects: expensive clothes, sophisticated computers, TV sets, music players, and fancy watches, which, in my view, were all substitutes for love. More interestingly, in his spare time he liked to invent things: smart, cute machines like gadgets that would put your toothpaste on your toothbrush for you in the morning. Or an alarm clock made of little toys. He was lazy and always hoped for a free ride, so all his inventions involved getting the greatest possible return for the least possible effort. Yet his mind was active and ideas poured out of him. He worked hard getting the plans for his creations down on paper.

I wanted to replace his bad habits with good ones. So I jumped on the inventing bandwagon and gave him assignments. I sent him to do research at the library and to get applications at the patent office. This was a long and arduous process, but he researched and applied for patents with a thoroughness and diligence that was impressive.

I then asked him to taper off his drug use. Doug went from tripping once a week to once every three weeks. Instead of using drugs regularly, he began to use them more recreationally. It was painful for him to stop, but I told him, "You have me to share your pain with now. You are no longer alone." In some ways I see every kind of substance that patients abuse as the same. The entire purpose of all addictions across the board is to repel depression and discomfort. Without the drugs, Doug felt sad, empty, and morose. But he was also more reflective, realistic, and philosophical. Within a year of therapy, he had stopped using drugs altogether. It was around that time he cried in front of me for the first time. These were huge breakthroughs.

The benefit of seeing patients at such a young age is that they are more malleable, not yet as set in their ways. It is easier to influence them than, say, an addict in his forties who has been using cigarettes or alcohol or marijuana as a means of coping every day for the last twenty years. The longer someone uses a substance, the more embedded his or her mistrust of others becomes and the harder it will be to stop. This is a good argument for early intervention.

Not long after he quit drugs, Doug was visiting a friend at a house he had burglarized. His friend's mother was telling the two boys how sad she was that her heirloom jewelry had been stolen. The missing pins and bracelets were presents from her late mother and grandmother and could never be replaced. For the first time, Doug felt enormously guilty for how his past misdeeds had hurt other people.

I thought his sense of guilt was appropriate and I did not discourage it. It was one of many complicated feelings I wanted him to face without turning to drugs. He went back to the pawn shop to retrieve her treasures, but they had already been sold. He began feeling regretful about everything he had taken from many different households and decided that he wanted to make restitution. This became his goal. He wrote a list of all of the items he had stolen. When he became a rich businessman, he said he intended to replace everything that he had taken. I sometimes encouraged guilt, especially when it motivates someone to become a better person.

"It's a noble mission," I told him. Yet I also warned him to be careful. By confessing his sins, somebody could decide to press charges and he could wind up in jail. That would not be the end of the world in my opinion, since he had broken the law and deserved to be punished. But he needed to be sure he was completely committed to the consequences of his recent, honest intentions. He said he was. He felt a strong desire to make amends. He saved up money and offered it to people he had stolen from, along with heartfelt speeches of confession and apology. Several neighbors told him to give the money to charity. Others were nonplussed by this kid wanting to atone. None pressed charges against him.

I continued to see him weekly for nine years. It isn't uncommon for a patient to quit his or her addictions quickly but then need much more time to unravel the huge, underlying problems that caused the substance abuse in the first place. Doug never went back to drugs or stealing. He improved his school work, went to a good college, and became better adjusted, getting involved with girlfriends and winning patents on some of his inventions. He is now a successful businessman in Manhattan. For a parting present he gave me a brass, antique pocket watch that was inscribed "To Fred, the father I never had."

Although of course not all addiction cases are so transparent, I find that all addicts share attributes I saw in Doug. Many people with substance problems feel empty because they have not been nurtured or fed well at home. They yearn to feel loved and cared for. Deep down that's what they are really after.

IMPORTANT QUESTIONS FOR AN ADDICT TO CONSIDER TO UNDERSTAND THE EMOTIONS UNDERLYING SUBSTANCE ABUSE

1. Growing up, did you feel loved? By whom?
2. As a child, with whom did you feel safest?
3. Was there anybody you could talk to who would help?
4. Who disappointed you as a child? How?
5. Who would you like to have been closer to?
6. What got in the way of your feeling close or understood by another person?
7. What did you miss the most growing up?
8. Was there a way you compensated for not getting enough love or attention?
9. Were those around you abusing food, alcohol, or other substances?
10. As an adult, do you feel safe?
11. In your present life, do you feel taken care of and loved?
12. In what ways would you like to feel more taken care of and loved?

CHAPTER 7

COMMIT TO STOPPING ONE ADDICTION AT A TIME: PROMISCUITY & ALCOHOL

"I'm just here because my parents made me come. They won't give me my allowance if I don't show up. But you better not fuck with me. All you fucking shrinks never did me a bit of good. You're all a bunch of white hypocrites in your coats and ties and fancy shoes," Erica said.

"Who told you that you could use that kind of language in here?" I asked her. "In this room, I've got news for you, you are a guest in my home. Things here go by my rules, including your language."

"This isn't your fucking home, it's your fucking office, and you're taking my money so I can talk any fucking way I want," she answered.

"I'm sorry, but I won't do this session until you apologize," I said.

"For what?"

"For your language and disrespect."

"Fuck you," she said.

I already liked her. I found her spirit engaging. It was our first session, in May 2002. Erica was a twenty-year-old, intelligent, pretty, light-skinned black woman from the Bronx. She was short, maybe five foot three, wearing overalls two sizes too big, a baggy overcoat, and sneakers. She appeared to be imitating a rap or hip-hop star's attitude.

Worried about her reckless behavior and substance problems, her stepfather had heard about me and insisted she make an appointment. She acted too casual, defiant, and well defended, which indicated she was hiding a serious problem. At this point I did not yet realize the extremity of her bad habits or what her primary addiction was.

"You are not listening. I told you not to use that language in my home," I said in the very firm, fatherly tone I used with my own children.

"Why shouldn't I use this fucking language in whatever the hell you call this place?" Erica asked.

I could tell she liked that I was acting so outraged. I sensed that she wanted somebody to see through her rough facade and set limits in her life.

"Because I don't allow it."

"Why?" she asked.

"Because when you're disrespectful, it hurts my feelings," I said.

She rolled her eyes. "It doesn't hurt your fucking feelings."

"If I say it hurts my feelings, it hurts my feelings," I told her. "Now I want you to apologize."

"I'm sorry if I hurt your feelings," she said, sounding somewhat sincere. Then she added, "But I'm not sorry for the fucking language because that's how I speak."

Now, I thought, I had her. Instead of her long, profanity-filled monologue, we were starting an interactive conversation. Erica had heard and understood me and compromised. Once she said she was sorry, I moved on. To dwell on behavior after an apology seemed punitive, and I was not out to punish or condemn Erica. I had a sense she was in big trouble. I wanted to win her over so I could help her out of whatever was so damaging that she needed layers of coolness and cynicism to cover up.

She spoke affectionately of her high-school-age-brother, Alex. Her mother, an Italian Catholic, worked at the Red Cross. Her biological father was a black Baptist carpenter, originally from the South. He had abandoned the family when she was six. Her mother had remarried a white businessman when she was twelve. They moved to the Murray Hill area of Manhattan. Erica did not appear to be close to her mother or her stepfather. When she was fourteen, her mother caught her smoking pot and threw her out of the house. She went to live with her biological father back in Crown Heights. He let her do anything and go anywhere she wanted; he was oblivious to what was happening in Erica's life. She alluded to bad habits and bad men. After a year, Erica moved back in with her mother with the promise that she would shape up.

"So you are like an orphan," I told her. "Or a street urchin in search of a parent."

"You're fucking crazy," she said.

Erica started seeing me once a week. She had dropped out of college, was not working, and made it clear that she showed up to our sessions only because she had to in order to get money from her parents. Her mother left many messages on my voice mail. "Erica stayed out all night last night. Did you know that?" she said. "Erica ran up the phone bill talking to who knows who." The next message was "Erica was getting stoned in our apartment when we were out, bringing strangers here. Do you know this is happening?"

Her mother's messages seemed demanding, expecting me to fix problems still outside of my sphere of influence. I was far from being able to control Erica's behavior in my office, much less in the outside world. On the other hand, at least this parent was showing concern for her daughter. She wanted to meet with me. After three months, partly to get to know the mother and get a better sense of what was really going on, I scheduled a session with Erica and her mother.

I knew from her therapy that Erica's mother was a significant figure in her life. She was also paying for Erica's therapy, so I felt she had a right to check me out. If her mother met me and left with a sense of confidence, she would keep supporting the treatment Erica needed. I felt this was important for Erica.

I was surprised that they did not look like they were from the same family. Her mother was white, thin, with dark hair and sharp features. She was dressed in more fitting and feminine clothes than her daughter. She was respectful and polite, giving off good-citizen vibes. Erica was also clean cut, yet she continued to speak with profanities and wear baggy clothes that hid her body and rejected any kind of female style.

Early on in their session, Erica did not understand something I said and asked, "What the fuck are you talking about?"

"You are not allowed to talk like that in front of me or your mother," I told her.

"It's okay. She can talk like that," her mother said.

"Not in my office she can't," I answered, getting the picture. Her mother had both kids when she was young, in her early twenties. She was a politically active liberal-democrat do-gooder. Yet she seemed too liberal with Erica. She established no restrictions or rules. I needed to be a role model in this regard for the mother, too.

Both Erica and her mother were worried that Alex, who was seventeen, was smoking pot as often as six or seven times a day. He wanted to get out of reality and stay in a dreamlike, buzzed state. Although Alex and Erica sometimes smoked pot together, Erica and her mother wanted me to help him. I was barely bonding with Erica, had just invited her mother into my office, and did not want to threaten our newfound connection by overconnecting with the entire family. Yet I was glad to see Erica so concerned for her brother; she had not walled herself off to meaningful connections. Often by the time I met an addict, he or she had turned profoundly away from people in favor of substances in order to experience relief. So it was good that human beings still mattered to Erica. I knew I'd caught her in time.

I recommended a Village Institute colleague as a therapist for Alex, who was flaky at first, missing appointments and forgetting to call. Eventually, with a year of good therapy that included more rules and accountability and a place to bring his angst and confusion, he quit marijuana and graduated from high school. He was easy. Erica was not. She was complicated, layered, and sometimes out of control like a wild animal who could explode with no provocation.

Although she had not yet divulged what was really going on with her, she never missed a session and always showed up on time—a sign she wanted to engage and to change.

"You're starting to like me," I told her one day, a few months into our therapy.

"I am not, fuck you," she said. "But you're different from the others."

"How am I different?" I asked.

"You tell me the truth so I know where I stand."

"Everybody else lies?" I asked.

"You do, too," she said. "You're no different. All you white guys with your fucking suits and ties are the fucking same. I know where you come from. You don't know me."

I was a "white guy" like her stepfather, whom she didn't like or trust. She had hostility towards both parents, who she felt were restrictive, uncreative, not empathetic. I saw it was easier for her to attack me than to feel close. Since her real dad—whom she resembled—had deserted her in childhood, emotional connections felt dangerous to her.

"I'm not just another white guy. I really want to know you and what's really going on," I told her.

"You have no idea where I've been and what I've had to do for money," she said.

"You're right. I don't know. So what have you had to do?" I asked. "Where have you been? Tell me."

"There's bad things you should know about me. You can't imagine," she said. "I've been arrested and institutionalized, locked in padded rooms. I've put my life at risk many times. I'm a fucking whore."

It took Erica six months to feel safe enough to admit that she had been having sex for money since she was thirteen. There had been more than 100 men in bars, clubs, private parties, urban rooftops, and on the street. She said she couldn't stop on her own, though she wanted to. She claimed that she did it strictly for the money; I knew deep inside that it was for the love and connection, however perverse that may have seemed. It was the worst case of sex addiction I had ever treated, especially because she was such a young girl. With my patient, Courtney, her mother's death explained the lack of supervision in her life that had exacerbated her promiscuity. But Erica's mother was alive. Where was she and Erica's stepfather while this was going on? I was once again dismayed that such seemingly responsible parents could be so clueless about their child's illicit activities.

My definition of sex addiction is that when you're not having sex, you feel unbearably alone and it's very difficult to stop. Sexual intercourse acts like medication, offering relief from utter aloneness and emptiness. So much so that life feels desperate without it.

Part of Erica's sexual encounters were facilitated by smoking, toking, taking other drugs, and drinking, which she'd started doing at twelve. I wanted her to get clean and sober, but I never tried to get anyone to quit multiple bad habits and stay off of them all at the same time.

If an addict has multiple addictions simultaneously, which is very common, I try to determine which is the most dangerous or life threatening of all of them. Drugs and alcohol alter your behavior and can lead to drunk driving, impaired judgment, and death quicker than say, cigarettes or overeating. If an addiction is putting my patient or his or her loved ones in danger in any way, that should always be addressed first.

With Erica's sexual acting out, the ramifications were enormously disconcerting. I pictured a host of terrible consequences for her indiscriminate sexual acts—AIDS, venereal diseases and other STDs, gang rape, violence, unwanted pregnancies and abortions, which might affect if she could have children in the future. It made me sad to think about the possibilities. Beneath Erica's external bravado, I saw a desperately lonely little girl. I feared she would really hurt herself or get seriously hurt or even killed. I wanted to protect her, as if she was an abandoned baby.

I know it's unusual for a therapist to acknowledge having such emotions. But I find addicts often have an infantile need for the attention and safety they never felt from their parents. They have turned to substances as a stand-in for soothing. So when they quit a substance dependency, they revert back to the age they were when they started using. A young and palpable hunger for love comes out. I felt that myself my whole life and I allow myself to feel those longings in my patients. I relate and empathize strongly. I often sense a patient unconsciously wants to be taken care of by me. In these cases, I keep up the traditional therapeutic boundaries, but often speak in a softer and more soothing voice, as if I'm talking to a child. I remembered that Erica had started using when she was twelve.

"Why do you sleep with strangers? They could hurt you. I don't want you to be hurt," I said.

"I'm just doing it for the money," she insisted.

There was a bit of sociopathy there: the ability to use other people for her own gain with no sense of guilt.

"I don't think you are having sex just for the money," I told her.

"Why else would I?"

"I think you want to have someone with you because you feel so lonely. But you don't want to admit it or get too close to anybody," I said. "So when you have sex for money, you can pretend it's impersonal. But you and I both know, it's also for the love."

This time she did not argue.

"You must stop having sex with strangers. It's not acceptable. You are not allowed to do that anymore," I said, emphatically. "It worries and upsets me. It is dangerous and beneath you. You could die. Please stop putting yourself in danger." I tried not to be judgmental but used a concerned, parental tone.

"Okay," she said. "I won't."

I was skeptical and said, "I hear you and I'm going to choose to believe you." I acknowledged that she might be conning me while allowing myself to hope she wasn't. Yet right after that, from all I could tell, Erica really did stop sleeping around. I had the feeling that she was ready to quit. She had been waiting for somebody in her life who cared about her to tell her to stop using sex so self-destructively.

I liked to think that with me as a constant in her life, she no longer had the same desperate need for a man's love and attention—because she had mine. Not that she would ever admit to needing me or to feeling close.

Obviously just saying "quit that behavior now" is not what usually works with addicts. Yet sometimes with my young female patients, it was easier to get results by being authoritative. With older males, there is the problem of pride. They often feel too humiliated to obey another man's orders. Some of the women I have treated seemed to have an emotional framework for submitting and yielding so that my being paternal did not compromise their dignity. I know it reeked of sexism, but my first goal was to do anything to get a patient to stop hurting themselves. I wondered if my demands would be met more quickly by women patients who were younger and virtually fatherless.

I realized that sometimes I was being sexist, demanding, eccentric, or bending typical psychology rules and limitations. Yet effective addiction therapy needed to be faster and harder hitting than regular psychotherapy. Remember, I had patients who would shoot heroin into their veins and then drive a car with their children in the back seat. Getting them safe and clean was my clear mandate.

From the way Erica explained it, it seemed that she craved intimacy like one would crave a substance. It soothed and filled her up the way alcohol or marijuana did. She enjoyed the rush and confidence her sexual encounters gave her. I surmised that when her real father had left home, she had felt like she had no control or no impact on him. He never took her feelings into account. Sleeping with men for money made her feel powerful. She could get close on her own terms and leave when she felt like it. She loved that they wanted her and that she could have them without revealing any emotional needs at all.

There was another reason Erica could stop her sex addiction before she could give up alcohol, drugs, or cigarettes. Out of all her self-destructive compulsions, having sexual intercourse often was the most complicated because it involved the cooperation of a partner. It would not be a control freak's preferred substance. Pornography or masturbation, maybe. But needing other people for your own satisfaction was troublesome. You could toss a beer can into the garbage, flush leftover pot down the toilet, stomp a Marlboro butt into the street, turn off your computer to leave an x-rated chat room instantaneously. Another person was not so easy to dominate, regulate, and get rid of. Underlying her sex addiction was a desire to get close but not too close.

As I often did, I asked Erica to keep a journal. I hoped it would give her another way of communicating with me (and with herself) that was not so personal and direct, something she could continue doing outside of my office any time she wanted. She soon gave up the need to be the tough girl and stopped swearing all the time. She started giving me copies of long stories she wrote, in stream-of-consciousness style, about herself and her past, often painful, day-to-day activities. Her writing seemed authentic, deep, soul searching, and emotional. I became a character in her pages. She quoted lines I said, then argued with my theories, referring to me, sometimes sarcastically, as "the good doctor." I loved it because it showed she was taking me in, taking me seriously, arguing with me in her head when I wasn't there. I took it as a compliment and a sign of progress.

"Did you read my story? Did you like it?" she asked in a childlike tone, like she ardently wanted my approval.

"It's fantastic," I said, giving her the unadulterated praise she longed for. "You've got enormous talent," I said.

She smiled the biggest smile. "Really? You liked it? You think I can publish it?"

"It's wonderful. But it is a bit undisciplined, like you," I told her, honestly. "Maybe you should take a writing class."

She seemed interested. Along with a part-time clerical job her mother helped her get at a local temp agency, Erica went back to college part-time, where she enrolled in English and creative writing courses. Yet, when they became difficult, she skipped classes and "forgot" to do her homework.

Periodically I asked, "Have you been having sex?"

"No," she said.

"How does it feel?"

"Horrible," she answered, which made me believe she was telling the truth.

"Are you lonely?" I asked.

"Fuck being lonely," she said.

"How do you stop being lonely?" I asked.

She looked at me and said, "I drink."

On the positive side, instead of one-night stands with strangers, she became involved with a few steady boyfriends. She demanded they treated her with respect. One of her boyfriends, a freelance handyman, was neglectful. But there was a nice, new, college guy on the scene I rooted for. She complained he needed her too much, which made her nervous. She brought in her writing almost every session. Erica became closer with her mother, who seemed to be getting more affectionate and open. In the last session they had together, her mother broke down and cried.

On the negative side, Erica continued drinking for two more years. When I asked the specific details, she admitted that she went out three times a week and would drink half a bottle of vodka or more. She would get sick and black out. Yet she was not ready to let down that shield, too. I brought up the subject of sobriety too often for her.

"Shut up already," she once snapped at me. "I won't come back anymore if you keep harping on my drinking. I'm sick of hearing you think I'm a fucking alcoholic!"

Rather than risk losing Erica as a patient, I decided to tone it down.

"Okay. I'll abide by your gag order and won't talk about alcohol," I said. "But I'll be thinking about it every time we talk. Because I worry about you. "

At Erica's lowest point, she came in with her face bruised and swollen. When I asked her what happened, she said, "Oh nothing, I ran into a truck."

"Back up and tell me exactly what happened," I insisted.

"I got drunk on vodka and was about to cross 3rd Avenue. I looked the wrong way for oncoming traffic, saw no cars, started crossing the street. A truck with a big mirror that stuck out whizzed by. The mirror hit me right in the face," she said. "I fell down, dazed. I was lying on the ground, thinking 'what am I doing, lying drunk on the ground on Columbus Avenue. What am I doing with my life?' It's pretty bad, isn't it?"

"I sure wouldn't want it to get any worse," I said. "Listen, Erica, how bad does it have to get before you let me help you stop drinking?"

"What do you want me to do?"

"Since when have you ever put yourself in a position to do what someone else wants you to do?" I asked.

"I know, I hate it. But I think I'm ready."

"Are you ready to follow my lead?"

I suggested she not have anything to drink for three days and see me on the fourth day. At my request, she began going to AA meetings every day. After ninety meetings in ninety days, she got a sponsor. She stopped seeing me in 2006 when I moved to Arkansas. When I last heard from her, I was happy to learn that Erica was back in college full-time and had stopped drinking.

IDENTIFY YOUR HABITS

Most addicts I see have crossover compulsions that overlap or play into each other. People who get drunk have lowered their resistance to other substances and are therefore more likely to sleep around, spend money they don't have, smoke, toke, or do drugs offered to them while they are inebriated. In fact, in my experience, it's rare for someone to only have one addiction. To delineate which habit you—or the person you are trying to help—should stop first, ask yourself these questions.

1. Does satisfying a specific habit involve seeing people with whom you would not normally associate?

2. Has your habit ever involved sleeping with someone you don't know well or respect? Or someone you regret seeing the next day?

3. Does getting your fix cause you to go to bad neighborhoods or stay out all night?

4. Does your habit involve illegal activity like stealing, selling drugs, or buying liquor underage?

5. Does your habit involve immoral acts like sleeping with someone married, underage or otherwise inappropriate, or not sober enough to make a good decision?

6. Do the people you associate with in order to satisfy your habit have weapons? Do they have prison records? Have they ever threatened you or mentioned past hurtful behavior?

7. Are you keeping what you are doing secret from everyone in your life? Has doing this alienated, angered, or upset your mate, members of your family, or close friends?

8. Are you driving while inebriated or on drugs or getting in the car of someone who is?

9. Are you taking care of children while under the influence or so preoccupied with satisfying your habit that you are putting them in danger?

10. Have you ever hit or harmed someone or done something illegal or immoral while getting or using this addiction?

11. While using this activity/substance, have you ever felt afraid for your well-being?

12. While using this activity/substance, have you ever threatened someone, verbally or physically?

13. While using this activity/substance, do you ever feel desperate and out of control?

14. Are you spending money you don't really have to satisfy this compulsion?

15. Does satisfying this addiction ever make you feel physically ill? (Passing out, blacking out, throwing up, dizzy, sick to your stomach?)
16. Do you ever feel self-destructive or suicidal?

If the answer to any of these questions is yes, I would highly recommend you:

1. Tell someone you trust what's going on—a relative, friend, classmate, workmate, teacher, neighbor, or doctor who has been helpful to you.
2. Find the phone number of an addiction specialist, therapist, or physician. You can do this through referral from another doctor or patient. Or, you can Google "therapist," "addiction," and your hometown and lists will pop up.
3. Call this addiction specialist, therapist, or physician and leave an honest, clear message that you need to make an emergency appointment ASAP.
4. Attend a group meeting soon. They are usually free, in every city, and around the clock. If you can't find the exact group you want, you might consider AA since many of the steps and tenets of all recovery groups are similar.
5. Look into the possibility of rehab at a hospital or facility you can afford, or your insurance might surprise you by covering it.
6. Take an empty notebook and pen and go to a place where you won't be as tempted to use and where you feel safe and comfortable—a park, your parent's house, an aunt or cousin or good friend's place, the library, a bookstore café, or coffee shop. Take deep breaths and write exactly what you are feeling for an hour.
7. Let yourself cry.

CHAPTER 8

THE SECRETS OF SOFT HABITS: BINGE EATING

One night after dinner, around 10:00 PM, I found myself feeling hungry and edgy. My wife and daughter were already upstairs, settled in for the evening. I went to the kitchen and took out the pint of Haagen-Dazs Vanilla Chocolate Chip ice cream from the freezer. It was my favorite flavor, and I was craving it. I turned on the television, sat down in my brown leather chair in the den, and spooned the ice cream right from the container to my mouth, forgoing a bowl. It tasted cold and soothing and I immediately felt better.

I started out thinking that I would have just a little. A single serving was 300 calories, well within the limits of my usually moderate diet. But by the second spoonful, I was already lying to myself. Or perhaps the self-deception had begun the day before, when I had purchased it at the deli, as I had a hundred times before. What had I been thinking when I picked up the pint? That I would eat just a little bit this time, though experience had shown that I had never been able to stop at just one serving, especially when I was tired from a long day of work and feeling stressed out late at night.

After consuming one serving, I still felt famished. I wanted more. So I kept going, blocking out all the information I knew—that eating an entire pint was a terrible choice for my diet, almost doubling my entire daily caloric intake. I pretended that I wasn't a little lactose intolerant and ignored the fact that I would feel sick tomorrow. I conveniently forgot that in my fifties I had to watch my weight or I would get a middle-aged spread like other male members of my family, which would cause me angst and discomfort. None of it mattered anymore because my brain had already flown out the window.

I knew the right thing to do would be to stop, but the idea of stopping now seemed ridiculous; thus, I might as well finish the whole thing. I had already ruined my diet for that day, so no further harm could be done, right? Faulty logic had completely taken over my thinking. I actually believed that eating the rest of the ice cream was going to improve everything in my life. I promised myself that I would eat much less food the next day, along with exercising vigorously to burn off the added calories. I actually felt entitled to this ice cream. I'd had a hard day and a rough life! This was what I deserved, what I never got.

The Greek dramatist Euripides had paid homage to the hedonistic Dionysius, whose philosophy was devoted to proving that life was nothing if pleasure was denied. Some part of me recognized that I was stooping to intellectual justifications to maintain my commitment to this pint of ice cream and to feeling this good. But I was in such denial at this point I could not tell the difference between what was real or what was a nonsensical rationalization.

I finished the whole container and went to sleep feeling sated. The next morning I woke up sick at 6:00 AM, kicking myself for my indulgence and feeling the inevitable food hangover. I weighed myself to find I had gained three pounds. I looked in the mirror and admitted my problem—I was becoming addicted to Haagen-Dazs Vanilla Chocolate Chip. Since I was six feet tall and a relatively slender 168 pounds, my ice cream compulsion was not as obvious a problem as the pack-a-day smoking habit I had given up. Nor was it commonly considered as serious as habitual use of crack, cocaine, alcohol, LSD, pot, pills, or gambling.

Still, I had slipped unwittingly into my old habit of using a substance to calm, soothe and reward myself, to regulate my emotions, and I was doing this against my better judgment. To stop eating the ice cream would have been difficult. It would have made me feel empty, anxious, or depressed. That was precisely why I knew I had to stop. I realized that the criteria for an addiction could now be applied to me. I had been exhibiting the typical addict's attitude that I was alone in the world, and I could handle everything myself. So I decided to treat myself the way I would treat a patient in addiction therapy.

Since I'm constantly advising my patients to "lead the least secretive life that you can," I took my own advice. Instead of hiding out downstairs with ice cream after my wife had gone to sleep, I spoke to her and to a few trusted friends about my ice cream foibles and the emptiness and anxiety that I recognized as the source of my cravings. I also made an appointment with my Jungian advisor, Bob. He helped me see that two particular areas were upsetting me in ways I had not realized.

After September 11, my wife and I had made a rational choice to sell our New York apartment, which was two blocks away from Ground Zero. It had been badly damaged in the World Trade Center attacks that hurt both my spouse and my daughter. Relocation seemed like a smart thing to do at the time, especially because the place had become filled with terrible memories of that day. But leaving the home we had painstakingly decorated and in which we all felt so comfortable was painful. It was draining and confusing to go through all the hassle and complicated emotions involved in selling our living space, packing up, and relocating. Our original plan was to rent an apartment and save money for a year or two before buying something else in Manhattan. We eventually decided to leave New York altogether and relocate to Arkansas. Although it was the right decision to better care for my family, that didn't mean there wasn't lingering confusion, hurt, and regret I had to contend with as well.

Along with the tribulations of recovering from the family trauma of being in the middle of 9/11 and moving from the city I loved, I had also been trying to reconnect with my mother, from whom I had been estranged since the 1970s. After almost thirty years of no contact, I had begun to send her flowers and small tokens for her birthday, Christmas, Valentine's Day, and any other holiday I could use as an excuse to mail her a present and a note.

After each gift, to my surprise, she began sending a handwritten thank-you card addressed to me at my father's house in another state. (Although they had been divorced for years, they were still in touch.) Yes, it was odd that my mother could not manage to send a note directly to my home. But her warm responses to my gifts represented meaningful movement forward for our relationship, as if a glacier was beginning to thaw. She was eighty-five years old and not healthy. I wanted to see her and decided to be more proactive, but I proceeded cautiously. After I sent the next present and received her thank-you card, I planned to drop her a casual note mentioning that I was going to be near her South Carolina home for business and hoped we could meet for coffee.

For the next holiday, Mother's Day, I sent her a basket of lotions and soaps, making sure the store put my home address clearly on the card. But her thank you note for my Mother's Day present never arrived at my address, nor my father's home. My plan had somehow backfired or stalled. As a psychologist, I could not help but analyze every angle of this latest rupture. Perhaps Mother's Day was too intimate and therefore too uncomfortable a holiday to recognize, since we had been estranged so long. Were soaps and lotions too personal a present? I feared that having included my home address with the gift had too implicitly demanded that she send her response to my own home, which was, in essence, demanding that she acknowledge me and my life.

Although the minute details of these transactions seemed trivial, they reminded me of the greatest source of sadness from my early years—that my mother had not loved me as a child. Is it any wonder that during this time, having given up the soothing action of smoking long ago, I now found myself reaching out for milk and sugar to help settle me and put me to sleep?

Although some might scoff at the idea that a basically thin, high-functioning, middle-aged man eating ice cream in his home could be heading for danger, look at all that was hiding below the surface of such a simple act. That is why I do not distinguish between "hard" and "soft" addictions. Whether it is a sweet dessert, Xanax, pot, nightly mint juleps, or too many weekend jaunts to Atlantic City, I have found that the specific substance or obsessive habit itself is of less importance than the chaotic and scary emotions that the substance is being used to regulate and repress.

Here is the reason why I could not ignore my ice cream escapades and why you should pay attention to every change in what you are consuming. Untreated and unacknowledged addictions never get smaller. They get bigger, spreading to other substances and activities or overlapping into more areas of one's life. Addictions rarely go away or dissipate by themselves. They must be acknowledged and understood before any treatment will be effective.

If left unchecked and unanalyzed, the habit of eating too much ice cream once a month will become once a week, and then will become once a day. I have seen such seemingly innocuous habits as running, viewing porn sites on the Internet, and even gum chewing lead to medical calamities, broken relationships, troubled finances, illegal and immoral actions, and the abuse of spouses, parents, and children.

The void that substances seek to replace can never be filled. So a once-a-week habit that seems to momentarily placate emotional emptiness can easily become a daily or hourly compulsion. Yet the quantity of what you reach for will only get bigger because the void is endless and won't be satisfied. Hence the necessity of getting off the merry-go-round to figure out what is really going on and let your sad feelings tell their own sometimes weird, complex, and long-winded story.

On Memorial Day, I went back to sending my mother flowers and more subtle gifts. She reverted back to sending her thank you notes to my father's address. I shared more with my wife, friends, and my advisor, Bob, about what was going on, and felt sadder, angrier, and more vulnerable. Yet I have not eaten any more pints of ice cream since then.

CHAPTER 9

THE HIDDEN PERILS OF ALL ADDICTIONS: CIGARETTES

Everyone seems clear about the bad health effects substances can cause. Smoking cigarettes leads to emphysema and lung cancer, eating too much junk food can make you obese, drinking large amounts of alcohol can damage your liver, driving drunk kills innocent bystanders. Yet what people tend not to see or understand are the more subtle and insidious effects of substance abuse, such as the way they can stunt your emotional growth and thwart your ability to discover new coping mechanisms for day-to-day difficulties. Negative effects are often so subtle that one does not realize what is being compromised by the use of substances.

Often my patients begin their treatment by revealing that there is something they want in their lives that they have not been able to achieve. Frequently it turns out, upon examination, that the secret force stealing their joy, success, creativity and the ability to really connect with friends, children, parents, and mates is the daily habit they don't even admit is a problem.

In the late 1990s, I was seeing a patient named Arthur, who wanted to quit smoking. Arthur was a forty-eight-year-old conservative, mild-mannered, white man from a Russian-Catholic family. He described himself as an architect working at a huge corporate firm that he hated, a faithful husband in a no-longer-exciting marriage, and a responsible father of a teenage son who was becoming rebellious. Arthur was melancholy, pent up, and repressed. At work, rules prohibited smoking inside his office. He would step outside to take cigarette breaks several times a day. There he wound up mingling with other smokers who worked in the same office building. He described the group of loyal nicotine addicts as kooky, artistic, rebellious types, like the kind of people he had worked with at a previous job that he had enjoyed immensely. His favorite part of his work day was hanging out outside with this motley crew. The most intense, intriguing people that the staid Arthur had ever befriended were people he had met because of his smoking habit. The challenge in his therapy was to separate him from his addiction, but not from the vibrancy that his habit appeared to have brought into his otherwise tedious, bland existence.

Smoking a pack a day seemed to be Arthur's most rebellious trait. It was the one way that he had burst out of his boring mold. Smoking embodied the creative, adventurous side of his personality. Not that I thought he should keep smoking. In addition to causing harmful physical effects, I believe that cigarettes—and all addictions—are emotionally damaging as well. Instead of having to struggle with negative feelings and develop creative and constructive ways to cope, smokers suck in the calming comfort of smoke that hides what is really happening inside of them. They artificially soothe themselves with a quick hit while stunting their long-term emotional growth and success. Like all addicts, they miss opportunities that could lead to expanding experience, understanding, and greater intimacy with others in their world.

For example, Arthur's wife hated the smell of smoke in their home. During weekends he would leave their apartment and go outside to have a cigarette alone, as often as ten or twenty times a day. So his habit interrupted the flow of his domestic life. He was not a full participant in his family; he was an outsider. When difficult or uncomfortable emotions surfaced, he would grab his pack of cigarettes and escape. He was puffing away his real problems, unaware of what they were. Yet by smoking he ensured they would remain the same because he was doing nothing to change himself or figure out creative ways to cope with the dilemmas that were bothering him.

Interestingly, at the same time I was also seeing another male patient, the complete opposite of Arthur, whom I was also trying to help wean off cigarettes. Khaled was a thirty-four-year-old single, Egyptian-born Muslim banker who had earned a graduate degree at Oxford University. He came from a wealthy, politically connected family and seemed sexist and classist. All the men in his culture and inner circle smoked cigarettes, he said, and he'd started as a teenager.

As repressed as Arthur was, Khaled was hedonistic, believing that his every sexual desire should be satisfied. He was vain, well dressed, often appearing for sessions in three-piece silk suits. The main reason he wanted to quit cigarettes was that he valued his physical prowess and hated feeling winded while working out in the gym. He was proud and arrogant and, unlike Arthur, hated to have to leave his office to smoke outside with what he considered to be the fringe people. Khaled wanted to be associated only with the CEOs. He was enraged at being asked to leave restaurants to smoke, like a second-class citizen.

Neither of these men wanted to use a nicotine-replacement therapy (gum, patch, nasal spray), nor would either attend any kind of group meeting. They were both stubborn and individualistic in different ways and wanted only to continue trying to quit smoking with me one-on-one. They both decreased the amount of cigarettes they smoked and increased talk-therapy appointments to two or three times a week. In these sessions I tried to shift their attitudes towards pain and the acceptance of the suffering they would need to go through to be smoke-free.

They also slowly changed their attitudes about nicotine, realizing that it was not helping them attain any of their goals. Indeed it was the road block *preventing* them from getting what they wanted. They both began eating healthier foods and exercising more. Based on my own slow and painful nicotine withdrawal after smoking for twenty years, I recommended such daily coping mechanisms as breathing exercises and taking a walk before shouting at somebody, amongst other techniques.

At first, when Khaled began to decrease the amount of cigarettes he smoked, he was irritable and short tempered, with low tolerance for frustration. But after a while, he became used to the withdrawal. The less Khaled smoked, the sweeter, milder, and more personable he was. He was becoming more three dimensional. For the first time he brought in Aimee, a woman with whom he was involved for six months, for couples sessions. He began calling me "Freddy." I tried explaining to him that in America that nickname was diminutive, even infantilizing, and could be considered insulting. But he insisted that in Egypt it was an affectionate term and kept using it. When he admitted to the extreme loneliness he had always felt, I began to feel a closeness with him for the first time.

Arthur was the reverse. Without his cigarettes, uncomfortable feelings that he had long ago rejected surfaced and he became increasingly volatile. He snapped at his wife and yelled at his son. Then he would weep with sadness, feel guilty for his impatience and intolerance, and apologize. Although he had always assumed he was "normal," Arthur soon discovered a range of anxiety, anger, sadness, loss, and rage inside him with which he had lost touch. Now a wider range of vivid sentiments and sensations were returning to him with a vengeance.

For Khaled, the cigarettes had hidden his gentle, endearing side. Conversely, Arthur's smoking had been squelching so much of his force and power that for two decades he had been only a shadow of himself. Both men were considered good-looking, hard-working, successful, law-abiding citizens. Yet their addictions were damaging them in similar ways—virtually wiping out entire sides of their personalities.

Compared to heroin, crack, or cocaine, a cigarette habit might be considered benign. Smoking is legal and one can buy cigarettes anywhere for relatively little money. Cigarettes do not impair your judgment or make you violent or dangerous. You can smoke and drive safely at the same time. Yet the cumulative unhealthy emotional effects of smoking in the nicotine-addicted patients I have seen have been equal to the physical threat of lung cancer and death.

There is a common misconception that alcohol, cigarettes, or drugs help loosen people up emotionally and sexually. These substances purportedly make painters, writers, and musicians focus better, go deeper into themselves, and produce more creative and original work. I have found that in most cases substances in fact do just the opposite. Addictions inhibit emotional intensity, artistic urges, and love. They act as blockades, often keeping users from being deeply involved with the people they care about or from becoming as powerfully creative and successful as they could otherwise be. After my patient, Kevin, gave up drugs and extreme sports, his business became more successful, he fell in love with a woman, and reconnected with his father. My coauthor, Susan, insists there's no coincidence that in the decade she's been smoke, drug, and alcohol-free, she has published eight books.

Not that my addiction therapy is always successful. During a couples session with Aimee about why Khaled was afraid to commit to marriage, I made a reference, too casually, to Khaled's fear of intimacy. This greatly offended him. He felt hurt and slighted and accused me of inappropriately revealing a confidence. I should have taken our cultural differences more into account and Khaled's extreme reluctance to be known and understood by me, let alone by me and a girlfriend simultaneously. He wound up quitting therapy. I regretted my mistake and often thought that if he stayed with our addiction work longer, Aimee's affection might have taken the place of his need to light up so many times a day. I heard from a coworker of his (who called me for an appointment for an entirely separate problem) that Khaled had gone back to smoking as well as to dating many women at the same time.

Arthur, on the other hand, remained in therapy and quit cigarettes completely. Although his smoking rituals had once seemed to enhance Arthur's creative streak, it was clear that nicotine had actually been washing him out, taking up space where more satisfaction could be experienced. Arthur did not leave his boring, but well-paid job after he quit cigarettes. Yet he did begin sailing and buying and fixing up old houses, activities which brought passion back into his world. He also became much more proactive about forging deeper relationships with his son and wife.

It does not matter if an addict in recovery becomes more likeable as Khaled did or more volatile like Arthur. These huge transformations proved to me once again that a person's most important energy is often tied up, and used up, by their substance. In giving up the smokescreen, you become less artificial and more authentically yourself.

ARE YOUR HABITS HINDERING YOU?

Many patients I have seen over the years do not believe that their habits are getting in the way of their relationships, personality, or their dreams. If you are not sure, here are some issues to ponder:

1. What do I want most in life? Am I achieving that?
2. What do I want most from a relationship with a partner?
3. Do I feel deeply loved day to day by someone special whom I trust?
4. Is there someone I adore in my life? Have these feelings been expressed?
5. What are my career, artistic, or lifetime goals?
6. What do I really want to happen that I can't make happen?
7. What is my biggest regret thus far?
8. Is there time to change it?
9. If I only had one year to live, what would be my main focus?
10. If I wrote my own fantasy obituary, describing what I'd accomplished in my life, what would it say? What would the headline be?

CHAPTER 10

LEARN HOW TO SUFFER WELL: OVEREATING, CIGARETTES

Last year at a dinner party, I was seated near an overweight man who was eating heaping helpings of roast beef, bread, vegetables, and potatoes. During the meal, when he heard me mention that I specialized in addiction therapy, he said, "I'm a food addict. I've tried everything—Weight Watchers, The South Beach, raw food, Atkins, low-fat diets. Nothing works for me." I looked at him and said, "Have you tried suffering?" He laughed out loud, as if I was joking. I wasn't joking.

Most addicts use substances because they don't want to suffer and hope to avoid feelings of anger, sorrow, pain and discomfort. In this regard, they are self-medicating with substances. However, life is filled with chaos and difficulties and there is no way around feeling hurt. Wilfred Bion wrote that mental health involved "suffering well" and that therapy should therefore be disturbing to the patient. A therapist should not strive to make you happy. Living well, even suffering well, are more attainable goals than being happy, regardless of what the advertising world, Hollywood, the Hallmark card company, and the pharmaceutical industry would have us believe.

The advertising gimmicks that we are continually fed contribute to our misconceptions about the cessation of addictions. Television commercials selling diet pills tell viewers that they can easily lose twenty pounds in two weeks. Exercise machine manufacturers imply that you can look like Brad Pitt and Angelina Jolie if you just use their contraption for ten minutes every night. Acupuncturists, hypnotherapists, and drug companies guarantee smokers that they can kick the habit after one (or a few) simple sessions or pills.

Some people with mild bad habits have been able to stop using with these methods. Maybe there is the unusual addict out there who can benefit from certain kinds of regulated diet pills, home exercise machines, acupuncture, or hypnotherapy. Yet usually these components work only if they are one part of a more comprehensive program designed by a recovery program expert, a doctor, or addiction specialist. Unfortunately, all these false promises perpetuate the myth that stopping substance abuse is a quick, easy process that leads to feeling good right after one has kicked the habit. In fact, almost always, it is exactly the opposite—you feel fine while you are using, but you will suffer and even feel sick when you quit—sometimes for as long as a year.

Getting rid of a long-term addiction is never going to be a one-step, simple process, especially if you intend to stay clean and not merely switch from one addiction to another. Studies show that most smokers who finally kicked the habit successfully had to quit five or six times first and that a large percentage of alcoholics and drug users relapse several times over the course of their treatment and recovery. However, Bion also believed that what hurts people most are secrets and lies, and what finally heals is honesty. One has to find a way to live *with* the truth, not fight against it. Alas Americans have learned intolerance for discomfort. Yet if you know in advance that you are going to be physically and emotionally uncomfortable, there are many ways to prepare yourself to make your suffering more bearable.

My coauthor, Susan, was shocked by how horrible she felt when she first attempted to quit cigarettes on her own. Since other former nicotine addicts she knew had been able to quit faster and with less trouble, she thought there was something wrong with her. It confused her that when she smoked, she felt fine. When she stopped, she felt sick—shaking, sweating, crying, overeating, and coughing up phlegm. She kept thinking the withdrawal symptoms would soon abate and it would get easier to quit. But, in fact, each attempt got harder, and she always ended up going back.

At her first therapy session with me, I gave Susan my standard warning: "You are going to feel like a hell for a year." During our subsequent weekly sessions, I explained my theory and methods further. She later said that my warning that she was supposed to feel like hell for a year was what helped the most. It made her feel like her reactions were normal and allowed. Since she knew in advance that she was going to experience twelve months of agony, she had time to prepare and change her plans, expectations, and outlook. In essence, she made room in her life for more agony and discomfort. This time stopping did not shock her or take her by surprise. She knew what to expect and made a specific, detailed plan for how she was going to cope with the onslaught of turmoil and discomfort that was coming.

Instead of constantly admonishing herself for how stupid it was to hurt so much, Susan decided to treat herself as if she was recovering from a serious illness (which, in essence, she was). She canceled draining meetings, charity obligations, and social plans, eased up her work schedule where she could, and asked her friends and relatives for their tolerance and understanding. When she had recuperated from an operation a decade before, she remembered that she had ordered in water, orange juice, and different flavors of low-fat sorbet. She had sat on her couch under the covers, listening to soothing Joni Mitchell music, watching reruns of dumb TV shows, and reading about the sexual escapades of celebrities in tabloid magazines for weeks with no value judgment at all. She felt she'd done nothing wrong and had been extremely kind to herself.

In order to heal from her addiction, she allowed herself to be similarly self-protective, selfish, and shore up all her energy. She took naps when she needed to, turned off her phone machine, and turned down stressful freelance assignments and family dinners with the excuse that she "wasn't feeling well." It was true, she wasn't.

Susan's strategy to quit smoking worked well. Instead of feeling stunned and overwhelmed with the amount of discomfort she experienced, she was pleasantly surprised to find that the worst of her physical and emotional nicotine withdrawal was over in nine months, not twelve. (Though each time she quit another habit, like Diet Coke, she had to re-experience withdrawal, but for shorter amounts of time.)

Interestingly, she found that part of her "selfish" quit-smoking strategy provided a road map for how to be more successful, take better care of herself in general, and to get rid of what Oprah calls "the disease to please." Susan has since incorporated this emotional self-protection into her daily schedule. She continues to take naps when she needs to, turns off her phone machine, and turns down stressful freelance assignments and family dinners with the excuse that she isn't "up for it," or that she's "overbooked." She is, since in order to stay clean and take care of herself, she knows she has to make downtime a priority in her schedule.

Quite often, addicts feel the worst exactly at the moment when they stop using, which is actually when they are the healthiest. They feel best when they are stoned out of their minds, which is when they are the most sick and most liable to hurt themselves.

One of my patients is constantly quoting cult author, Tom Robbins, who said, "It's never too late to have a happy childhood." I disagree. I believe that people use substances to soothe themselves in the way they should have been calmed and soothed in their formative years. Unfortunately, it is too late to make up for what one did not get as a child. Ultimately you cannot go back to your childhood. For adults, the window of opportunity for that kind of maternal nurturing has closed, and there is no soothing mommy who will come back and take care of you. Using substances in order to soothe yourself does not make you feel better in the long run. They make you feel worse, like waking up sick and weighing more after eating a pint of ice cream in one sitting.

Addicts who are in pain and discomfort have come to me wanting "to feel better." Yet a substance abuser is in deep trouble exactly because he or she wants so much to "feel better" that he has had to use unhealthy substances or activities to achieve that goal, which is never sustained for long. Substances succeed in self-medicating only for short periods of time. A common misconception about addicts is that they are hedonistic pleasure seekers. This is not the case. Most addicts I have seen do not use to seek pleasure. They are people out to avoid terrible pain. They use not for fun, but often just to feel okay and get through the day.

A recent book by neuroscientist David Linden, *The Compass of Pleasure,* argues that the scientific definition of addiction is actually rooted in the brain's inability to experience pleasurable feelings. According to Linden, a Johns Hopkins University School of Medicine professor and editor of the *Journal of Neurophysiology*, variants in genes turn down the function of dopamine signaling within the pleasure circuit. For people who carry these gene variants, their muted dopamine systems lead to blunted pleasure. While most people achieve a certain degree of pleasure with only moderate indulgence, those with blunted dopamine systems are driven to overdo it, Linden explains. In order to get to that same set point of pleasure that others would get to easily—maybe with two drinks—an addict needs six drinks to feel the same way.

Linden argues that understanding the biological basis of pleasure leads to rethinking the moral and legal aspects of addiction. It also underscores the importance for addicts to not react according to their feelings, but instead follow rules and guidelines to help them get—and stay—clean.

WAYS TO EASE QUITTING

If you want to end an addiction, here are some changes you might have to make to protect yourself while you are going through all the difficulties of withdrawal and recovery.

1. **AVOID TRIGGERS:** All addicts have different things that set them off and make them want to use. It is essential to recognize and remove an emotional or actual real-life trigger whenever possible. If you are attempting to stop drinking alcohol, do not go anywhere near a bar, a wine tasting, or a fraternity social with a keg. If you are a gambler, cancel upcoming vacations to Las Vegas and Atlantic City—or a trip to anywhere that has gambling of any kind associated with it. If you are on a diet, avoid pizza places, bakeries, and ice cream parlors. You can ask hotel concierges to remove the candy or alcohol in their mini bars before you get there and waiters to take away bread baskets in front of you. Indeed, avoid restaurants altogether for a while, especially eateries with fattening foods and buffets you used to love. Nobody has sufficient willpower to resist temptation when repeatedly confronted with it face to face, especially while in withdrawal. Do not try to test yourself in this regard because you will lose or add so much stress to an already enormously stressful situation that you will end up relapsing.

2. **STEER CLEAR OF "TOXIC" PEOPLE:** The people you live, work, and socialize with will have a huge impact on your success or failure quitting a substance. Make a list of everyone in your life, including partners or lovers, friends, colleagues, and relatives. Now next to their names, write down your guess as to whether they will be part of the solution or part of the problem. Does being with this person make you want to use for whatever reason? You have to ask yourself, when you are with them, is this person going to be on your side, understanding, helpful, and supportive in your quest for sobriety and health? Or are they going to try to undermine you, even without meaning to have that negative effect on you.

    You might think you don't have the answer to this, but deep down you do. The first obvious question is: do they still smoke, drink, gamble, overeat, or do the drug that you are trying to stop? Or are they going to encourage you to use, even with the best of intentions? Spend the least amount of time possible with those who are using the substance that you are trying to quit or with those who have any investment in your continuing to use along with them. This will be especially difficult when it includes a relative or close friend. If it's a parent, sibling, adult child, or someone you simply must have contact with, you might consider such alternatives as email, the phone, faxing, teleconferencing, and snail mail instead of seeing them in person.

If it's your boss or coworker, you may even have to explore the possibility of getting a new job or being transferred to a different office or floor. In some cases, you may also be able to look into different shifts or flexible hours or see if you can work part-time from home. Your first response to this might be "that's unrealistic." I'm sure that's what the late British singer Amy Winehouse told anyone who suggested she get out of the music business for a while until she quit drugs and drinking.

3. **TAKE TIME OFF:** There is a reason why rehab centers work. That's because addicts leave all the complicated problems in their lives behind to focus all their attention, for one month or more, on getting better. Even if you can't afford Hazeldon or have a job or children for whom you are responsible or prefer not to go away, there's still ways you can chill out and give yourself a break. Consider taking your vacation time or taking a sabbatical or leave of absence. Had Amy Winehouse remained in rehab longer, she might not have been found dead of an overdose at age twenty-seven.

4. **MATE DEBATE:** If you're trying to diet and your spouse overeats in front of you, this can be a serious impediment to your success and may cause marital problems. Consider seeing an addiction specialist or couples therapist together. If your partner is not ready to diet along with you, consider going on a solo vacation or a yoga retreat. When you get back, you can discuss the rules that would help you, such as: no junk food in the house.

Don't eat candy in front of me. Don't sabotage my efforts. Eat pizza out with your friends when I'm not around and don't talk about it in front of me. If your partner truly cares about you, he or she will be glad to cooperate and help.

In extreme cases, where a couple both abuse alcohol or drugs, I have sometimes recommended separation, or even divorce. I know that sounds extreme. Yet I remember when Tiffany, a former heroin addict I once treated who was clean for ten years, went back to using because her husband left drugs around their home when he fell off the wagon. No matter how much Tiffany loved him, she knew she could not risk her life and health when he was unwilling to change. She is now on her own, sad but drug-free again, and in a new job and apartment, while her husband is out on the streets.

Also read about the recent Medford, Long Island, pharmacy murder when Melinda Brady, a woman with an addiction to hydrocodone, spurred her husband, David Laffer, to murder four people in the course of a robbery to get her fix.

5. **LIMIT TIME WITH YOUR EXTENDED CLAN:** You may think you are obligated to spend Thanksgiving, Christmas, New Year's, July 4th, and every birthday and anniversary with your relatives, but you can easily change that. Family get-togethers are regressive in their very nature because everybody returns to their old roles. Parents become parents; children become children, no matter their chronological age. It will be difficult for an addict to adhere to new, healthy rules and regulations in that setting. You must take care of yourself first. Treat your addiction like a disease, realize you are sick and at risk, and protect yourself from all triggers and people who add stress to your life. If you drink, smoke, toke, or overeat every time you are in the presence of your parents or in-laws, either don't go or come up with alternatives. You can stay at a hotel instead of at their home, for example, or lessen the amount of days or hours you spend with them.

Lisa, a patient of mine, deconstructed why she always over-ate and drank too much at family events. The two-hour com-mute to her parents' suburban house, and her mother's buffet, were the specific stress inducers. She stopped going, but invited her family to meet her instead at a health food restaurant in her neighborhood. Although they were hurt by her absence at first, her clan finally agreed to join her. Instead of an eight-hour ordeal, this gathering took only two hours. She hugged every-one goodbye outside the restaurant, did not invite them over to her place later, and did not overeat or drink. Later she called to thank them for coming and expressed how happy it made her that they came to her neck of the woods. It has now become a yearly ritual that has made them all closer and healthier.

6. **FOCUS ON SLEEPING BETTER:** Sleep deprivation will lower your re-sistance to all substances and make quitting nearly impossible. Sleep must be considered an essential component of stopping any addiction. Discuss with your therapist any changes you can make, at least for the short term, to get better rest. Ask your spouse to cover for you or even consider hiring a nanny or babysitter to get up with kids in the middle of the night or early in the morning. Redesign your bedroom to make it easier for your to sleep. (Some prefer pitch black, others prefer using a night-light.) Take out TVs, exercise equipment, toys, and everything else but the bed. If the bed you have now is not big or comfortable enough, consider buying a king-size or Califor-nia-king-size mattress and box spring. Buy silk sheets or a new comforter as a present to yourself.

7. **WATCH ALL CONSUMPTION/ACTIVITY MORE CAREFULLY:** When you quit a long-term addiction, your entire system is bound to change. Even if you stopped smoking and alcohol is not your problem, cutting down on alcohol will help you get better. If you are having trouble getting enough sleep (an important weapon in your recovery) you may have to cut down on caffeine or least avoid it after 5:00 PM. Be careful of tea, soda and chocolate—

hidden sources of caffeine. Try not to eat anything after dinner. Although exercise is good for you, finish your workouts several hours before bed. Make sure that you don't begin to eat, drink, gamble, or shop more to overcompensate for the substance you have lost.

8. **FIND SOOTHING RITUALS:** This can be different for everyone, but when you're feeling stressed out or anxious, consider taking a warm bath, listening to your favorite Mozart music, getting a massage, painting, or reading a special book under the covers. You have to start taking care of yourself the way you wish someone else would take care of you.

9. **TAKE ADVANTAGE OF THE RECOVERY SYSTEM:** Although you might feel alone, Alcoholics Anonymous, Narcotics Anonymous, and many other offshoots provide a huge national organization that understands exactly what an addict goes through. There are free meetings with like-minded souls available many times a day in almost every city. You don't have to commit to going regularly or to telling your own story to feel safer in the presence of people who get it.

CHAPTER 11

THE IMPORTANCE OF THE RIGHT SOCIAL LIFE: PAINKILLERS & FOOD ADDICTION

While socializing can be the very thing that encourages the use of substances one is trying to quit, many addicts I've seen go to the other extreme. They cut themselves off from the world of people—with all of its beauty and its dangers. Isolation encourages secrecy and shame, which a healthy social life combats. As we saw with other patients, you can be the wrong kind of busy and superficially popular and still feel desperately lonely. Yet when someone removes themself from all normal social interaction, bad habits can become impossible barricades, as they were with Marsha.

"It's completely ridiculous that I'm calling, since I'm already seeing a psychiatrist. But since I love doctors so much, I figure one more can't hurt," was the message Marsha left on my Manhattan answering machine in the spring of 2000. Her voice sounded knowing, humorous, self-mocking. I thought, "She has to be feeling too much pain to even discuss."

On a first message, most patients say, "Something bad is going on," or "I'm feeling freaked out and drinking too much." Marsha's upbeat tone seemed phony, as if she was trying too hard to be amusing. To be fair, I had other reasons to think this as well. She had been referred by an oncologist at an upstate cancer center where she had

119

been diagnosed with a slow-growing kind of leukemia. "It will kill her but there's no saying when" was the gist of his prognosis. He was stumped when she refused the chemo he recommended (which could have lengthened her life by ten years) and ignored his warning that she was taking way too much antianxiety medication.

This oncologist had previously recommended a patient who had been given one year to live. With medical treatment aiding her physically and therapy helping her emotionally, she survived for seven more years, more comfortable and stress-free than her doctor had originally thought possible. Medical doctors often recommend psychotherapy to lower stress, which is considered to be very helpful in treating a compromised immune system. Also, addiction to pills and pain medication is rampant and continues to grow. According to the White House Office of National Drug Control Policy, the number of people seeking treatment for abuse of prescription painkillers rose 400 percent from 1998 to 2008. Unfortunately, most physicians do not specialize—or even have a cohesive plan—for getting patients to stop overusing such substances, even when the use of these medications worsens their illness.

Marsha showed up half an hour early for her appointment the next week. Since on the phone she'd sounded very crisp and put together, I was surprised to find an obese forty-five-year-old with messy brown hair and no makeup wearing a baggy beige outfit. Her clothes were too big on her, as if she were hiding her body. She seemed very anxious.

"Tell me about yourself," elicited a twenty-minute, nonstop monologue of her physical ailments. She claimed she could not walk down the street without becoming dizzy. She had vertigo and had to hold on to parking meters so she would not faint or fall down. At every step, she feared she would fall or have a heart attack and die on the street, alone. She listed her physical symptoms with no clue that any of this might be psychological. When I asked why she would not get the chemotherapy her doctor suggested, she said, "There's no point. It's hopeless. Why should I fight?" She was passively suicidal.

Living alone in Queens, Marsha had never married, cohabited with a partner, or had children. She had grown up in a reform Jewish family with no siblings. Her parents, who had never shown any love for her, she said, were dead. She was profoundly lonely and always had been so. She had a college degree but had worked for more than a decade as a receptionist at a Manhattan company. Although she seemed agoraphobic, from nine to five she had perfected a cheerful false facade at her job in order to make a living and survive. The only thing she seemed to enjoy was food.

"I wake up in the morning, go to work, come back to my apartment, and eat. I don't go out again until work the next day. That's my life," she said. "Don't interfere with it."

I felt her admonition was serious. Postcollege she had never lived with another person and seemed deathly afraid of the prospect of continual interaction with another human being. Her obesity and fear of any kind of intimacy made me suspect there had been trauma in her past, but she shut me down whenever I asked. At the same time, she was unhappy; she must have wanted to open up and change or she would not have kept coming to my office. As defensive as she was, over the next few months Marsha told me I was "growing on her." She came early, wanted to stay after our sessions ended, and even once admitted, "I don't want to leave."

"I bet it's difficult to leave a place that feels safe with someone else when you haven't been in a such a place for a long time," I told her.

"So you understand," she said, then added, "But don't think that's going to get you anywhere."

In many ways Marsha remained reserved and had trouble revealing anything private. She seemed both terrified and intensely desirous of being close. It's a paradox not uncommon to addicts who crave closeness but often give up on people in favor of substances, which are less likely to cause disappointment and are much easier to control.

Addiction usually involves secrecy and denial. Debbie, another female patient, asked me if her candy binges were a real problem since she wasn't overweight and she indulged only monthly. When I offered the criteria of lying and covering up as part of a litmus test, Debbie admitted that she never ate junk food in public. Instead she would wait until her husband was asleep and then sneak to an all-night drugstore to buy $5 worth of chocolate and red licorice, which she ate quickly in the dark by herself. She would not even leave the wrappers in her own garbage; she carefully disposed of them in the incinerator down the hall. Interestingly, on the nights she binged she rejected affection from her husband, even avoiding his embrace in bed, feeling "fat, gross, and guilty" as if she had cheated on him with candy. Debbie eventually gave up sugar and found when she and her husband ordered in pizza and overindulged together, she would eat less than she did alone and not feel as bad or bloated afterwards.

Often sneaking around and hiding is intended to camouflage an addict's behavior from others, as well as from himself or herself. That's why it is so important for addicts to have core pillars in their day-to-day world who encourage them to open up and compromise emotionally, even when it's uncomfortable or annoying.

Early in our therapy I asked Marsha where she worked, and she refused to tell me. If I pushed her, she warned me, she would lie.

"I probably wouldn't recognize the name anyway," I said. "But hiding everything in your life is bad for you. Can you try to be more open and vulnerable, even if it hurts? If you can't find one person in your life to trust, you won't get better. So I think you should consider telling me where you work."

"Okay. I'll tell you," she said, mentioning the name of a business I had never heard of.

"Why should I believe you?" I asked.

"You shouldn't. I'm lying," she said.

I kept at it. Finally, she told me the name of another company.

"You look so uncomfortable now. On that basis, I believe you," I said. "See, you took a risk and nothing bad happened."

"Not yet." She smiled.

"Obviously you are afraid to feel close to me or anyone. Or have me feel close to you."

"Don't even think about it," she snapped.

Instead of a social life, Marsha visited myriad physicians—oncologists, internists, and Dr. Zelner, an uptown-Manhattan psychiatrist she'd seen weekly for fifteen years. She had insurance covering the doctors and tests at the hospital, but her other appointments and medications were breaking her. Adding a regular session with me would cause financial hardship.

"If you see me weekly and you are brave, it will be worth your money," I said. "If you see me once a week and you act like a coward, it will be a waste of your sacrifice."

"I guarantee you, I'm a coward," she said. "So don't get your hopes up."

Marsha was very smart, witty, humorous, and feisty, yet her life was a disaster. Still, I liked her. I always liked shipwrecks. That was how I used to see myself, so I identified with those whom no one could help. Since I believed I had triumphed over the complete wreckage I could have become, it was easier for me to be optimistic with other lost souls. Although every shipwreck requires its own unique salvage plan, I knew that in cases this extreme, one had to rebuild from the ground up. That's what I had to do to recover from my own disasters: my mother cutting me off at nineteen, leaving my wife and Long Island job when I was forty, and having my home destroyed on September 11, when I was forty-eight.

I wondered if starting over was like Freud's theory on repetition compulsion, where you master your initial trauma by reliving it, each time with a better end. Maybe starting all over again is an opportunity to live differently and make better choices than before. More conservative therapists have criticized the way I use my past to connect with my patients, yet I embrace my history as a resource for deeper empathy. I hoped my experiences with addiction, family abuse, and reinvention might help Marsha come up with a less tragic ending to her story.

Marsha said she was taking the tranquilizer Ativan, the sleeping pill Ambien, beta-blockers for hypertension, and a goulash of antianxiety medications for which she had prescriptions. She was using fifteen or more pills a day, none prescribed by her cancer doctor, which confirmed to me that her pill use had become an addiction. She was also constantly overeating. Since nothing she was doing was immediately lethal, and you cannot take a substance away from an addict without replacing it with something else—often a different way of coping—to fill the huge void, I did not at first ask Marsha to quit or cut down on her substances. Instead I tried to establish more of a connection between us. She did not make that easy, reiterating all of her medical problems every single time I saw her, sometimes for the entire session.

"Do you have any idea how tedious it is when you do a monologue listing your ailments?" I asked. I didn't want to be mean or insensitive, just honest. I would not have been as blunt with someone fragile or delicate, but I felt Marsha could handle it. She did not need to be patronized. The truth was what engaged and helped her.

"Do you think that's why Dr. Zelner's eyes close during our sessions?" she asked.

"Yes," I answered. "During your litany of complaints, my eyes could be closing, too."

She laughed. "Thank God somebody else is as bored with my illnesses as I am."

"If Dr. Zelner is always falling asleep, why do you still see him?" I asked.

"He's one of my addictions," she said.

It sounded like Dr. Zelner was not trying to get Marsha to stop self-destructive behaviors. For fifteen years, he was essentially holding her hand, even while falling asleep. He seemed to be adhering to the public health policy of harm reduction, not demanding abstinence, trying to be encouraging rather than judgmental. Having the steady human contact was good for her. At least it got her out of the house once a week. If a patient was in AA or group therapy or had another doctor he or she liked, I rarely discouraged it. A recovering addict needs a support system. The more the better.

Yet I am not the type of therapist to hold a patient's hand with no improvement year after year or be mild and patronizing, even for one session. When it comes to addictions, I disagree with the harm reduction theory because I find very few addicts can handle using moderately, and in my experience, addictions do not stabilize on their own. Untreated, they only grow worse. Marsha needed to be pushed into medical treatment soon or she would die of cancer. I felt therapy that went deeper and challenged her would be much more effective.

After a year of seeing Marsha I told her, "Part of you has given up. It is just you and the pills and food. That is all you have. Yet here I am breaking through your defenses, confronting you, making you reveal yourself. And you keep coming back, which means a small part of you has not given up."

"Do you think that's why I call your answering machine every day to listen to your voice and find it so reassuring?" she asked.

This surprised me. It seemed an apt metaphor: she was calling but never leaving a message. I didn't have caller ID and my machine did not record hang-ups, so I had no idea. "Yes, you obviously want to get clean, buy yourself more time with the chemo, and feel less alone and more connected to me," I told her.

"Well, don't get a swelled head over it," she said.

"I do not often fail, and I do not intend to fail with you," I assured her.

"You are going to fail," she warned.

"I want you to commit to trying four things, though it will be difficult," I said.

"No way. I can't. If you keep this up, I'm out of here," she said. "What four things?"

I outlined my plan. Since I believed good addiction therapy should be goal oriented and incorporate behavioral strategies, I often constructed specific, individualized, and idiosyncratic, steps. There was not an exact science to what worked with my addiction patients. It was trial and error. In this case, since Marsha's only core pillars were me and Dr. Zelner, I encouraged her to join Weight Watchers. She desperately needed a sense of community that did not involve just work or her doctors. Weight Watchers was a group that could provide human contact and compassion, as well as help in weight loss and healthy eating.

Second, I advised her to go out to a movie every weekend and report back to me what she thought of each film. It seemed important to get this patient out of her apartment. She was a highly intelligent and articulate person, and I guessed that she would enjoy analyzing and talking about movies she saw.

Third, I suggested Marsha buy a locket with enough room to fit an Ativan pill inside. I wanted her to wear it around her neck and to think of it like an emergency fire extinguisher. I explained that if she dissolved Ativan under her tongue and then swallowed it, she was guaranteed to experience relief within thirty minutes— she could even time it to see it work. It was completely reliable. Since she knew she could always open up the locket, take the pill, and feel relief within half an hour, I hoped that this would comfort her so she did not have to take many of her antianxiety medications preemptively every morning, and that the Ativan in the locket would help her tolerate more anxiety than she dared expose herself to thus far.

I warned her that my fourth suggestion might seem absurd. I instructed her to always walk on the north side of the street when she was going east or west and to listen to my voice in her head, reminding her to crossover over to the north. At first she said that was impossible, since she forgot about me altogether as soon as she left my office. But I insisted that this was not about me; this was about always walking on the north side of the street. I knew that Marsha, like most addicts, suffered from a lack of sufficient parental love. That meant she had few healthy internalized voices on which she could rely. Instead she needed an external substance (whether a glass of wine, cigarette, pill, cocaine, or candy bar) to get through the day. I wanted Marsha to think about me (a symbol of sanity, care, and concern) instead; I would be the external substance. Focusing on which side of the street to walk on was a way of making sure that she would always hear my voice, a caring person's voice, in her head, and that she would remember that I existed.

"Can you just try it . . . for me?" I asked. "I think it might help."

"Okay. But I wouldn't do it for anybody else," she said.

"So did you give my plan a shot? How was it?" I asked at our next session.

"I can't believe this north side of the street stuff is working," Marsha reported. "For some reason it makes me feel much better, thinking about you all the time. Though I hate to tell you that because it will just feed your huge ego."

People who aid and abet addicts (like dealers, enablers, and fellow users) become like their family. Luckily so do those who help a substance abuser recover. Physicians, sponsors, and recovery group allies can become intensely connected to an addict's internal addiction cycle, affecting the neurotransmitters in the brain that control pleasure. I encourage this deep overlap during treatment, even if good results are motivated by the power of suggestion or an addict's sheer devotion to his or her sponsor or doctor.

Indeed, Marsha reported back that my plan, odd as it was, calmed and inspired her. She was seeing movies and discussing them with me. She was wearing the "Ativan locket." She was walking on the north side of the street. Within two months she was able to cut down from fifteen pills a day to one, which she thought about carefully before taking. Since she had suffered from serious panic attacks in the past, I conferred with a psychopharmacologist who agreed that one pill a day had a medicinal effect and was not feeding Marsha's addiction. It was the equivalent of an AA member in a car accident who needed morphine at the hospital. Sometimes a substance can be medicine when taken legitimately and nonaddictively, although this is difficult for many addicts to pull off.

Marsha sometimes went as long as a week without taking even one pill, which I considered a triumph. Without so many pills she was less tired and depressed. She said she felt more agile and had more energy. Although it was still hard to push herself to come see me, once she was in my office, she seemed delighted to be there. She loved telling me jokes, making me laugh, and sharing self-deprecating stories about how hard it was for her to master bus routes and subway stairs.

Getting her to go anywhere but work and therapy and weekly movies was difficult. In winter, Marsha feared she'd slip on the sidewalk and break her hip. In summer, she was afraid she would sweat too much or die of heat stroke. Still, despite her discomfort being in public, she managed to go to Weight Watchers meetings three times a week. Over the next year, she lost forty of the hundred pounds she needed to lose. This reduction at first made her feel elated and successful.

Unfortunately, as she lost more weight, the elation and success scared her. She admitted it made her feel attractive and sexual for the first time in years. That frightened her because her instinct was to hide herself completely. Marsha said she felt she was too exposed, as if her whole nervous system was closer to the world that terrified her. So she quit Weight Watchers and gained back twenty pounds. We explored her anxiety therapeutically, as she'd been doing for fifteen years, yet without medical treatment, her time was running out. I didn't want her to regress by gaining all the weight back and returning to her pill addiction. Every session I encouraged her to go back to the meetings and her oncologist.

"I can't. Stop pushing me," she said. "You're going too fast."

After four years of seeing me, Marsha finally did get chemotherapy for her leukemia—a major, albeit late, breakthrough. At the same time she decided to quit our therapy. When I asked why, she said, "I feel too close to you. I don't want to start feeling good and then have to say goodbye again each week. It's just too painful." I realized she had become too vulnerable with me without enough other pillars to balance our closeness. She needed more real people in her life and more substitutes to lean on.

She did keep calling, sometimes leaving me messages. I called her back each time and said "When are you coming in?" She refused, saying she was too terrified to come back to my office because then she'd feel closeness and would have to leave again. A year ago, she asked me to meet her on the steps of a brownstone near my office. I did. She said she went back to taking some antianxiety medication but was no longer addicted to food since she'd lost her appetite from the chemotherapy. Her old friends and coworkers complimented her weight loss.

"Cancer has its benefits," she joked.

I found it tragic that she never resumed our therapy because she had made so much progress. Had she gone back to Weight Watchers—even just for the company—I believe she would have become healthier and more connected to the world. Those weekly meetings could have made all the difference. The Weight Watchers community may have been the closest thing to a healthy family she ever had.

In retrospect, I could see mistakes I made with Marsha. Taking away fourteen antianxiety pills a day and a large portion of Marsha's food intake after the first year of our therapy was too much deprivation too fast. Two doctors as core pillars and going to the movies by herself was not enough to compete with the constant support the food and pills had provided.

After a patient who did drugs for twenty years told me, "I don't feel ready to stop," I said, "You'll never feel ready. Quitting will always be an extreme shock to your system." No addict ever really wants to give up a soothing crutch and in doing so let him- or herself feel terrible pain. That's why he or she often has to hit bottom or be pushed to stop. On the other hand, my biggest error with Marsha was being so impatient and frustrated with her lack of progress that I imposed my wish for her to stop her addictions before she could stand the deprivation and deal with the loneliness left in its wake.

That's always a danger in addiction therapy. I think "if only this patient would stop using he or she would be so much better off." It's hard not to try to persuade addicts to quit a habit prematurely.

Although she still refuses to see me in person, Marsha still phones my voice mail every day. Just last week she left a chatty message on my machine that ended, "Don't call me back." When I did call her back, as I always do, she laughed, clearly glad to hear from me, and said, "Oh my God, I can't believe it's you! Why are you calling?"

WHERE TO FIND PEOPLE TO ENHANCE YOUR WORLD

Along with doctors, one-on-one therapy, and recovery groups, here are other places where you can find colleagues and comrades to improve your life and well-being:

1. **TAKE A SEMINAR, CLASS, OR ENROLL IN A CONTINUING EDUCATION PROGRAM:** Whether it's film, cooking, knitting, stand-up comedy, or creative writing, many college extension classes are anywhere from two to sixteen weeks, and all kinds of undergraduate, graduate degrees, and certificate programs take several years to complete. That offers a long-time period to connect with classmates and teachers. If you are low on funds, scholarships might be available, as well as space for those who prefer to audit a course for no credit.

2. **TRY RELIGIOUS SERVICES OR ORGANIZATIONS:** It doesn't matter if it's as reform or orthodox as you are. What matters is your comfort and connection level. You might even enjoy services or activities associated with a religion different from yours. Susan, who is Jewish, joined Hadassah and Ort, where she met several female rabbis and other women from her tribe that she admired. But she became closest to an Episcopalian reverend at Holy Apostles Church, where Susan was volunteering. She wound up feeling more comfortable there than her family's long-time *shul*.

3. **JOIN WORK ORGANIZATIONS OR ACADEMIC GROUPS:** It's often free or inexpensive to become part of a larger network and there are many benefits including discounted services, event invitations, and connecting with like-minded people. So consider joining a chess club, the local PTA, your condo or co-op board, or your alumni association. When Susan reconnected with NYU's alumni group and joined for $30, she was asked to give two campus lectures and from there wound up planning free readings and panels at NYU's new bookstore, a beautiful 20,000-square-foot space two blocks from her home.

   Also consider a professional union or association. I am a member of the American Psychological Association, the New York State Psychological Association, and the Psychologists of Northwest Arkansas, as well as a member of my alumni associations. For writers, Susan recommends the American Association for Journalists and Authors, the Authors Guild, the Writer's Guild, the National Book Critics Circle, and Friends of the Public Library.

4. **ARTISTIC ENDEAVORS:** Many local schools, theaters, and libraries offer a range of productions, theater, dance and music recitals, readings, meetings, and programming that's free or low priced. Barnes & Nobles across the country have many weekly author events, as do independent bookstores. In New York, for example, Housing Works Bookstore Café has dozens of fun events open to the public and all proceeds from book sales go to their AIDS charities.

5. **SPORTS TEAMS AND CLASSES:** Consider joining a baseball or volleyball team, a bowling league, a bicycle club, a weekly spinning or yoga class. It will get you out of the house, the exercise is great for you, and you'll meet people you otherwise wouldn't to be on your team—literally and figuratively.

6. **VOLUNTEER AND SUPPORT CHARITIES:** Although a flurry of different activities might be meaningless, weekly one-on-one time with those in need can be soul quenching. Offer to be a big brother

or big sister to a lonely child in your city, feed hungry people at a soup kitchen, bring elderly people meals on wheels, or visit sick children in the hospital. These are marvelous ways to meet other kind people and keep good karma circling.

CHAPTER 12

QUITTING AN ADDICTION EVERYONE LOVES (AND ENCOURAGES): GAMBLING

"This is Jim Brody, calling for an appointment. Sally, my fiancée, heard about you from Adelphi, where she's a student. She thinks I drink too much though I don't really think it's a problem."

That was the message Jim left for me in May of 2000. I recognized the voice of denial, central to addictions. Many people call me and say, "I don't think this is really a problem." Well, nobody calls a therapist without a good reason. By leaving a message the caller implicitly, but unconsciously, admits he needs help. Often, however, his conscious mind then denies it. Patients I've seen are rarely aware of the contradiction, especially addicts, who hate to admit dependency on anything or anyone. They are the most likely to call with "no problem."

The psychoanalyst Wilfred Bion felt, "A main function of a therapist is to create a problem." That is, one of the first tasks of an analyst is to define and articulate the patient's issues as he sees them. According to Bion, if ones does not know what the problem is, one cannot find the solution. This is one reason it is so important to first determine if someone has an addiction. If you don't have an accurate picture of the conundrum, you can never fix it.

Jim was twenty-four, a successful, Jewish, Wall Street trader from a middle-class, Orthodox family. When he first showed up at my office, he was wearing cutoff shorts, unlaced sneakers, no socks, a baseball cap on backwards, and a sloppy T-shirt with a sophomoric "I'm With Stupid" slogan. He was dressed like a twelve-year-old. No successful adult had ever come for a therapy session with me clad so casually and inappropriately, like he was ready for volleyball on the beach. I've been accused of being judgmental when it comes to clothing. Maybe so. But I am trying to read externals in order to accurately diagnosis deeper issues of which the patient might not be aware. In this case, I sensed that Jim's attire revealed essential truths about his psychology. He appeared to be a hedonistic, impulse-driven, rebellious rule breaker who was avoiding the responsibilities and the pain of adulthood. "I wear what I want to wear," his clothes shouted. "I do whatever I want to do. Regular rules do not apply to me."

All addicts are impatient, have significant difficulties delaying gratification, and cannot control their impulses. Jim had an obvious impulse disorder. More comfortable in shorts and sneakers, he could not even tie his laces, tuck in his shirt, or put on a pair of pants for a meeting. As a trader on Wall Street, he said he always dressed like this, even though he had been made a vice president at his firm and had his own office. He was oddly shy, humble, and quiet and became animated and electric only when he talked about his work. It turned out this sloppy slacker was surprisingly one of the world's most successful traders, already worth many millions of dollars.

Paradoxically Jim's biggest problem was that the money he earned justified and validated his unhealthy, childlike habits. I've found the more successful and wealthy an individual, the more others tolerate antisocial behavior that is bad for the person's mental health. Think of the fortune Charlie Sheen made while he was addicted to drugs and prostitutes and how abusive he was to women in his life (he "accidentally" shot his then-fiancée Kelly Preston in 1990). His behaviors were not only tolerated, but handsomely rewarded with money, status, press, and fame.

In accepting Jim's eccentricities and immaturity, society was doing him a tremendous disservice. I didn't care if a friend or relative dressed casually, preferring to be comfortable. Yet as a psychotherapist, when a patient blatantly broke normal conventions, it told an important story that I heeded. By living the way he wanted to live, Jim's relationship with Sally was falling apart and he had no idea why.

"I have a few beers with the guys once a week after work to chill out," Jim told me. "I'm not an alcoholic."

"If your fiancée is upset by your drinking, then no matter what, we already know that alcohol has become a problem in your life," I told him. I explained that the technical criteria for addiction involves its interference with one or more major areas of your life—intimate relationships, physical health, social connections, family ties, and professional functioning. Jim was going out drinking with his buddies instead of spending time with the woman he was going to marry, thus creating a chasm between them. Since she had already declared that his drinking disturbed her and he seemed to love her and want to protect their relationship, his intimate world was already compromised by alcohol.

"But I don't drink that much," Jim argued. "Sally is wrong."

"Even if you only drink a few beers a week, if your closest relationship is compromised because of alcohol, then it's a problem in your world."

Like most addicts, as I suspected, Jim was consuming much more alcohol than the amount he first mentioned. He was drinking five or six beers, along with straight vodka, at least three nights a week, coming home drunk. As he slowly reduced his alcohol intake, Jim became more hyper and edgy. I began to speculate that he had been self-medicating an attention disorder. I sent Jim to my psychopharmacologist colleague Dr. Sands, who diagnosed ADHD and put him on a small dose of Concerta, which had a dramatically calming effect. Jim seemed to get more engaged in therapy, asking questions, eager to relate long stories about his past.

Although he described his parents as loving, they barely seemed to have noticed that he drank and gambled his way through college. Indeed, it soon became apparent that gambing was another one of Jim's addictions. Many times a year he went to Las Vegas and Atlantic City with coworkers. They spent the weekend drunk and playing Twenty-One, Roulette, rolling the dice around the clock, often losing tens of thousands of dollars. He used gambling to take him out of himself, the way other addicts sniffed cocaine, smoked joints, or tripped on acid. With gambling, excitement reigned and rational thought flew out the window. The sensation made him feel omnipotent, as if he was in a trance or could control the cards or dice. Jim was addicted to the thrill of the thrill. It was a high that constantly took him out of himself, removing him from any negative or uncomfortable feelings that he might otherwise have had to face.

The way Jim described it, a son in a Jewish family who legally made millions could do no wrong. There was a permissiveness and subtle neglect in that logic. An addiction that is socially and culturally endorsed and rewarded is difficult to treat. Confusingly, it became clear that the main arena where Jim's gambling addiction flourished was at the job that had made him a millionaire and so socially acceptable. In stock trading Jim gambled legally all day long.

Jim's extreme, self-made success was complex. The president of his firm was also a modern, Orthodox Jewish and graduate of the same New England college as Jim and gave him a lot of leeway. At their Wall Street firm, Jim would win or lose large sums of money all at once. Though winning provided a quick thrill and often gave him hero status around the office, Jim could see the dark side. Addiction always has a dark side. At one point Jim came in very upset that a twenty-five-year-old colleague, distraught over losing several million dollars in a trade gone wrong, had shot himself.

This death rattled the president and all the employees of Jim's company, who had long been worried about the high level of depression, anxiety, and substance abuse in their line of work. Jim gave the president my number and he called to ask me to come to the trading company to provide grief counseling after his young employee had ended his life. I could tell this could be an all-day affair and I didn't want to cancel sessions with ten regular patients who had appointments. So I sent two colleagues from The Village Institute. They spoke to the traders about the perils of addiction in their business and then saw employees one at a time to provide both grief and personal counseling. Along with feeling relieved they had someone to talk to, several of the traders wound up toning down their most ambitious trades, deciding certain risks weren't worth the agony they might cause. Several went for more sessions, intrigued by my promise that if they drank less and did less drugs, their focus would be sharper and they would make more money at work.

When this turned out to be true, the president was so pleased he wanted to have a psychologist on call for his employees twenty-four hours a day. I suggested that he hire a psychologist to work on-site full-time, at the cost of $100,000 a year. When he hesitated, I said "You go up and down more than $100,000 every hour. Why don't you gamble that a good psychotherapy program will stabilize your employees, reduce substance abuse in your firm, and increase your profits every day?"

He agreed and the firm hired a full-time therapist we provided who worked under my supervision. Part of her job was to develop an elaborate set of rules and guidelines to steer traders away from the addictive psychology and towards trading more rationally. For example, if a trader lost more than 10 percent of a stock, he was not allowed to say, "I just know this will go up," and get himself into further trouble by depending on Lady Luck. Instead he would have to cut his losses. The essence of the plan was: do not trust your feelings and do not rely purely on luck. Instead depend on a well-thought-out system. Indeed, using our strategy, the firm's profits went up considerably and the staff seemed healthier and less prone to extreme emotional damage and out of control mood swings.

The minute the president of his company hired an on-staff psychologist, Jim felt validated and delighted and loved blending his

two surrogate families (at his firm and The Village Institute). He
acted as if I had received a gold seal of approval. I was kosher. He
committed to seeing me once a week and opened up more. Seeing
me no longer meant he was a neurotic patient who needed a shrink
for help. Now he was merely a member of a business firm seeking
advice from a mentor who had become a bona fide part of that team.

Jim refused to go to AA meetings, but he committed to twice-a-
week therapy. He was worried that his older brother, Ben, had a serious alcohol problem and asked if Ben could come to see me, too. I
saw Ben three times. He was a forty-year-old divorced theatre owner
who was a raging alcoholic, drinking a bottle of vodka or more every
day. Although alcoholism can be genetic, I guessed that since Jim
looked up to his older brother, he had unconsciously emulated his
drinking. The first two times Ben saw me he was drunk and late,
barely able to remember where my office was. I asked him to try not
to drink before our next session and intentionally made the appointment for 9:00 AM, but Ben couldn't. He showed me an open mini-
bottle of vodka he'd already half finished that he had bought on his
way to our morning session. He missed our next appointment and
Jim called to tell me Ben had died of alcohol poisoning. I felt badly
that Ben had not come for help sooner, since by the time we met it
was clearly too late.

Ben's death shocked and changed Jim, who was afraid that his
own drinking and gambling jaunts were out of control. He asked if
he could bring in Sally, his fiancée, now a social worker. She seemed
pretty and normal, in a neat skirt and blouse, nothing sloppy or outside the box about her. She was more religious than Jim, mentioning
that she kept Sabbath and a kosher home. I noticed that as Jim spoke
to me, he looked over at her often, wanting her approval; he clearly
loved her and was here to address her fears that his coworkers were a
bad influence on him. We worked out ways Jim could socialize without alcohol or gambling. He would meet his colleagues for breakfast
or lunch, but committed to having an early dinner with Sally six
nights a week and seeing her on weekends.

After one year, Jim quit drinking altogether. After two years, he also stopped his jaunts to Atlantic City and Las Vegas. He married Sally and they now have two children. They became involved in their local temple. I suggested Jim consider a different line of work entirely, for the same reasons I would tell an alcoholic to stop working as a bartender. Jim refused to even consider retiring or switching professions. But he did give up working full-time and restricted himself to trading on his own for two hours a day. Even with this abbreviated schedule, he continued to make more than $1,000,000 a year.

Jim started playing basketball at a local court. A lot. Sometimes for hours at a time because he didn't have to think when he played; it seemed to relax him and clear his mind. It's typical for an addictive personality to get off one addiction by becoming addicted to another. Yet playing basketball was better than drinking and gambling. It was not an extreme sport that often lead to injury, so I didn't discourage it.

Jim replaced drinking and gambling with four things: family, religion, basketball, and therapy. He still has trouble controlling his impulses and gets distracted easily. He's a ragtag patient, missing appointments or coming late. Over the years, I have learned that with addicts, I have to expect the unexpected. Many patients miss sessions, ring my bell at times when they do not have appointments, sometimes come to sessions drunk or stoned. When Jim makes an appointment for a couples session with his responsible wife, he and Sally always come right on time. When he is supposed to see me alone, the odds are 75 percent that he'll show.

IDENTIFY HIDDEN ENABLERS

Although Jim's case study may appear extreme, it illustrates several of the perils and paradoxes that an addict must face when getting clean.

1. **KNOW THAT SOCIETY OFTEN REWARDS BAD HABITS:** A five-foot-ten-inch actress or model who weighs 110 pounds might be offered

lucrative film and TV roles or print and runway work. Yet that is not enough weight for her height, and she might be starving herself or overexercising to maintain such a low body weight. Similarly, an athlete on an award-winning team might be using steroids to increase his speed or performance. Coaches, agents, managers, team owners, and even friends may turn a blind eye to unsafe practices that "benefit" such professionals. Money and external prizes should not color your decisions or outlook. Addictions always turn out to be dangerous for the user, whether they are misguidedly rewarded or not.

2. **DON'T FOLLOW YOUR GUT:** I know we are all told to trust our instincts, but often an addict's instincts are wrong and will lead him or her back into using, excess, and denial. In Jim's case, his instincts at first told him he did not have drinking or gambling issues when it would be obvious to any neutral observer that he had serious problems. He called a therapist only at the insistence of his fiancée, who was a graduate student in social work and recognized that Jim needed help much faster than he did.

3. **DON'T ASSUME ACHIEVEMENT IS REDEMPTION:** In this country, people think that having an impressive title, awards on your shelf, or a big bank account indicates some kind of inherent goodness or god-blessed productivity. That is not the case when it comes to substance abuse. Quite often the sacrifices one has to make in order to achieve so much are unhealthy and downright dangerous. Sometimes success breeds greed or behavior patterns that lead to the misconception that you are above the law. Think of Michael Jackson, Tiger Woods, John Edwards, Ivan Boesky, Kenneth Lay, Richard Nixon, Martha Stewart, and Joel Steinberg. The list of the mighty who have fallen is endless. An addiction therapist can help you find strategies to stay honest and humble. It is possible to achieve and maintain success in the real world and be healthy at the same time.

4. **PARENTS DON'T ALWAYS KNOW BEST:** Jim's parents thought he was a wonderful, successful son who, in their eyes, could do no

wrong. They did not know how much he was drinking or gambling. It turned out that Jim's older brother, Ben, also a wealthy businessman, was an out-of-control alcoholic and cocaine addict. There is never one single reason why somebody engages in substance abuse. Many health professionals think there is a genetic component to addiction. While this may be true, I do not believe genetics fully accounts for substance abuse problems. Yet meeting Ben reinforced my feelings that something systemic was wrong in this clan. The two sons appeared to be loved and accepted automatically because they were boys and had lucrative, seemingly impressive careers. I guessed that they were not actually understood for who they really were inside as individuals. Their parents were not abusive, but there was intense neglect in the home and an unwillingness to delve too deeply into anything that was dark or not socially acceptable to discuss.

5. **SAY NO TO "YES" MEN:** Although your fans, underlings, and entourage might not want to rock the boat, fawners and hangers-on who flatter you are not good for your mental health. Beware spending too much time with students, acolytes, protégés, and people who want or need something from you. They are often not in a position to tell you the truth or provide tough love or guidance.

6. **YOU NEED ETHICAL ADVISORS YOU RESPECT:** Whether it's your grandfather or another older relative, a clergy member at your church, temple, or mosque, a beloved teacher, or a present or former boss, you need to find people you admire who will set a moral example. It's best if you can find someone who could spend time with you one-on-one, answer questions, and discuss any personal dilemmas you might be having.

7. **FIND ADDICTION MENTORS:** All addicts trying to stem their substance abuse need the right mix of support, honest criticism, and reality checks. This can best be provided by a therapist, drug counselor, or sponsor who will often be the only person

to argue, challenge, disagree with, and point out distortions in your logic. This is partly because we are unbiased outsiders who are not emotionally involved in your day-to-day life. We do not need your love or approval and have little stake in your decisions. In fact, the healthier you get, the more successful your addiction mentor will feel. It is therefore in our interests to point out your problems directly and to get to work on them efficiently.

There is an episode of the Emmy award winning television drama "The West Wing" where Adam Arkin plays a blunt and provocative psychiatrist treating President Bartlet. The show's writers underscore the reason why a good therapist can be so essential for somebody feared and admired. It is especially important for patients who are used to being fawned over and patronized to find somebody who is not intimidated by money, fame, or power. You need to find somebody you trust who will not be afraid to tell you the truth. And you need to listen. Your life might depend on it.

CHAPTER 13

BEWARE THE SUBSTANCE SHUFFLE: PIERCINGS, TATTOOS, OXYCODONE

"Sorry, I had to get the tat. I was too excited," Jordan said, showing me the Camus quote burned in her arm. "I love this one so much. I needed to get it finished."

Jordan's excitement and her inability to postpone gratification gave away the fact that she had become addicted to body art. I had asked her to wait five days longer to get another tattoo, but she couldn't. She sounded very passionate about adding a twentieth "tat," as if it was the only source of pleasure in her life. She was showing more emotion towards the decorations on her skin than she expressed for the fiancé with whom she lived.

Jordan was a smart, talented, twenty-three-year-old aspiring painter with long, brown hair who worked part-time in a pet store; she loved animals. When she first started coming to my Arkansas office in March of 2008, she was neatly dressed in jeans and a tucked-in knit top, well coiffed, and charming. "How are you today?" I asked. Each session, she would smile and say, "Fine. Good to be here. Everything's cool." But it was clear everything was not so cool. She was anxious, her feet shaking with restless leg syndrome, and she complained of crippling migraine headaches that no doctor or medication could stop.

The first addictions she revealed were Oxycodone, Vicodin, and codeine. After her mother had caught her with pills, Jordan had gone to rehab where she gave them up. But the minute she quit taking pills, she started drinking (wine, beer, scotch, and vodka) and smoking cigarettes. She was a polysubstance abuser who also told me, "I'm really into body modification."

"What do you mean by that?" I asked.

"My torso is covered in tats."

I could see a little skull and bones on her palm and a raven on the inside of her arm, yet it was winter, so the others were hidden by her clothing. "Define covered," I said.

"From my shoulder to below my waist is all tattooed." She clarified that there was only empty skin because some of her tattoos weren't finished yet.

I hadn't realized that Jordan had already tattooed her legs, feet, hands, arms, neck and chest. She said there was a fertility symbol from Greek mythology on her thigh, a native American emblem on her back, and a garden of Eden mural on the entire right side of her body. Jordan agreed to cut down on drinking and within a month had given up alcohol. But from what she told me, her tattoos were spreading.

I admit I'm a bit prudish when it comes to body art. I'm usually not afraid to be outspoken with a patient, but with Jordan, I kept my opinion to myself. I didn't want her to see me as another dumb, disapproving, parental person who didn't get it. I would be of more help if she trusted me and thought of me as someone who understood.

Over the next few months, I asked her to stop the process of filling every inch of her body with "art" until we could better understand what was motivating her. I was relieved when she agreed to slow down. But then she became obsessed with piercings on her tongue, ears, navel, and lips.

During the next week, she told me she had cut her arm and legs with a razor. With the few patients I'd seen who were cutting themselves, they were looking for an act that was so painful and, therefore, so focusing that all their other bad feelings disappeared. I urged Jordan to commit to twice-weekly therapy, determined to uncover what extreme emotions inside her were causing such extreme external actions and reactions.

After a while, when she'd come in and say, "It's good to see you. Everything's fine," I would say, "You don't have to act so cheerful and polite in here. We don't have to pretend. Let's face it: everything is not fine." She slowly opened up more about her sadness and feelings of isolation. So when I'd ask, "How are you?" she'd answer, "I'm miserable. Nothing's going right but I don't know why." She called her parents "heartless," admitted she was unhappy living with her fiancé, and had no real friends. She blamed herself for being "a fraud" who never revealed who she was to anybody.

For the next four months, Jordan's bad habits were slowly replaced with twice-weekly therapy, antianxiety and sleep medication prescribed by a doctor, and weekly massages and acupuncture, which I hoped might soothe her holistically. Over time, with these healthier substitutes, she said she was done with Oxycodone, Vicodin, codeine, alcohol, and cutting and that she was taking a break from getting further tattooed and pierced. I was gratified we were making progress. Until she came in enthralled with a new plan: piercings on what she called "her private parts."

I looked it up on the Internet where it said that having genital piercings done at a questionable shop could cause many medical risks, such as infections, HIV, hepatitis, allergies, and nerve damage. Truthfully some of the pictures made me ill, but I tried to hide my squeamishness from Jordan.

"Can you wait a few weeks, until we can talk about it more?" I begged her.

But by the next week she'd already had a procedure done. "Sorry, couldn't wait. It was like asking a child to postpone Christmas," she told me.

This was an unusual and challenging case that disturbed me. Jordan's switching around with so many different compulsive substances and activities was a terrible sign. It seemed a graphic representation of how out of control she was; there was no respite. The painful waste-land inside of her was being externalized. She couldn't stand living in her own skin and her internal chaos was seeping out everywhere. I feared the excessive body modification crossed a line because, unlike most addictions, it was permanently disfiguring and virtually impos-sible to undo. It was as if Jordan was sentencing her flesh to forever be frozen in this twenty-three-year-old despairing time.

Jordan agreed to a joint session with her mother, who wanted to get the bottom of why her daughter had developed so many extreme habits. She was a lawyer; her husband was a builder. Jordan grew up in a middle-class home as the oldest of three children. Her parents were still helping Jordan out financially. There was no history of de-pression or anxiety in the family, no genetic predisposition to addic-tions I could find. It seemed Jordan had never been abused, hit, or traumatized by any specific incident. Her parents stayed married and said they'd always loved her. They both worked a lot, so I wondered if inattention had fueled their daughter's loneliness.

"What's wrong with her?" Jordan's mother kept asking. "Where does it come from?"

Jordan would have been easier to treat if I could have pinpointed that she'd been stuffed in a closet for a week at four years old and that specific trauma had shocked her into using addictions to escape the memory. But I found no smoking gun. No obvious abuse or neglect. I had to dig deeper. Like her parents, Jordan's siblings had conven-tional jobs—her brother was an accountant, her sister a teacher. I guessed that Jordan's artistic sensibility made her feel like an outsider who couldn't fit in anywhere. She didn't feel "seen" for who she really was. The extreme multiple tattoos and piercings seemed rebellious yet hidden, secretly shouting that she was different, that she wanted to be noticed.

Yet if Jordan stopped piercing, cutting, and using alcohol, cig-arettes, and pills, I feared she'd find something else to excite and distract her, to take her out of her feelings. This hopping from one addiction to another is so common I call it "the substance shuffle."

Although all the addicts I had seen across the country tended to use multiple substances, the habits themselves seemed to vary by region. Since I'd moved to Arkansas in 2005, my patients were mostly white Christians (Baptist, Catholic, or Methodist) whose cross addictions tended towards alcohol, meth, Oxycodone, and other prescription drugs. Several had multiple tattoos; it seemed a more accepted practice in the South. In New York, I saw many Jewish and Muslim patients and people of color. My East Coast patients were more likely to be addicted to alcohol, cocaine, ecstasy, marijuana, and pornography, sometimes adding sex addiction into the mix.

The biggest difference I noticed was that in Arkansas many of my patients were ashamed to be in therapy or even to walk into my office. At a function for my daughter's school, a woman came up to me and whispered, "I have an embarrassing personal secret I want to reveal to you, but promise you won't tell anyone."

"I promise," I said.

"I'm in therapy . . ." she told me.

"And?" I waited to hear this horrible secret she'd been dealing with in treatment. It took me three more times of asking to figure out that having a therapist *was* her big secret! I told this woman that in Manhattan, those who came to my office were more ashamed *not* to be in therapy and would say things like, "I know it's ridiculous that I haven't been seeing a shrink regularly."

Over thirty years of practice, I rarely saw an addict anywhere with just one bad habit. Sometimes alcoholics seem only to like to drink. But if you scratch the surface, you'll often find they also smoke or need daily caffeine or develop sexual compulsions or eating issues when their resistance is lowered by alcohol.

All substance abusers suffer from an impulse disorder in which the switch doesn't turn off when it's supposed to. Addicts tend to be impatient, have extreme difficulty tolerating feelings, and cannot control their urges to flee from the painful emotional landscape inside them. Once a specific addiction has ceased, if you don't deal directly with the underlying emotional problems that caused it, you'll simply switch addictions. That's why you see so many smokers stand outside AA meetings puffing away. Research in substance-use disorders has shown that the prevalence of smoking is estimated to be as high as 80 percent among treatment-seeking alcoholics. Patients who quit cigarettes often get dependent on cigars, pipes, marijuana, and hash. Many former addicts gain twenty pounds after they quit smoking, toking, drinking, or pills, merely switching their drug of choice to food (hence the expression "sobriety weight").

Although studies in neuroscience have shown how compulsive sex, drug, alcohol, and nicotine addictions all share the same neurobiological pathways, sometimes the link between addictions initially appears to be less obvious.

When my patient Courtney quit using cocaine and having reckless sex, she became hooked on buying expensive clothes. Since she could pay the bills, she didn't see it as a problem. Yet shopping perpetuated the same mind-set and behavior as her cocaine and sex addictions. She had trouble saying no to the strange man propositioning her and then she couldn't say no to the salesgirl trying to sell her goods she didn't need. Using cocaine and buying frivolous $350 purses were distractions from her pain. Both activities excited her, took her elsewhere, provided an escape. While I didn't want Courtney to simply switch bad habits and pretend she was getting better, purchasing excessive clothes she could afford was better than coke and sleeping with strangers. So I didn't immediately tell Courtney to cut up her credit cards. You can't quit multiple addictions at the same time. And although I usually aimed more for abstinence than harm reduction, sometimes downgrading habits from dangerous to innocuous was a great improvement.

Still, during recovery, you must monitor your habits. I warn patients to beware of all excitement (like shopping, gambling, sexual connections) because when you are excited, it takes you out of yourself and you always eventually have to return to who you are and live with yourself. Although Jordan had stopped taking pills, drinking, and cutting, she continued smoking and maintained her fascination with body modification. She seemed to view the pictures and piercings that adorned her flesh not as artwork (as I'd initially suspected an artist might), but as friends who made her feel less alone, as if they were always there to keep her company and stave away her loneliness. It reminded me of the security I felt when I kept a cigarette pack in my pocket. Checking to make sure my smokes were still there made difficult emotions more tolerable. Similarly, Jordan merely had to look down at the picture adorning her hand, foot, elbow, or stomach to feel comforted.

Jordan, who was more visual than verbal, was not interested in keeping a written journal or diary, no matter how many times I asked. But it seemed to be a breakthrough when she offered to share her artwork with me.

"I make pretty still lifes and flowers. Is that what you want to check out?" she asked.

"No. I don't want the pretty stuff. I'd rather see your darker work," I said.

"Are you sure? It's kind of heavy," she warned.

"That's the only work I want to see," I reassured her.

She started emailing me photographs she'd taken of her paintings that were dark, morbid, and tortured, filled with swirls of black and gray skulls, ghosts, and pale people in the corners who looked like they were in agony.

"What do you think?" she asked, looking nervous that I might be as mortified by her ghoulish images as her family was.

"They are incredibly communicative," I said. "Complex, dark, and very important."

"What do you think they communicate?" she wanted to know.

"How you feel haunted, broken apart, in pieces, and can't put yourself back together again," I ventured.

She started crying, looking sad and deeply relieved at the same time.

The closest I came to understanding the roots of her pain was during a mother-daughter session. Jordan, upset and disheveled, mentioned a rough commute getting to my office because the Dalai Lama was in town and several roads were closed. I said, "Jordan is having a bad day." Her mother turned to her and truncating her daughter's experience said, "But it started off as a good day." Jordan responded, "You're right, it did begin good."

In that second, I got it. I felt like I was watching this well-intentioned mother—who only wanted to hear what was good—convince her daughter not to express any bad feelings. I realized that all of her life Jordan would repress and deny her difficulties to please her parents by saying, "You're right, Mom, everything is fine," then go take drugs, get a tattoo, or cut herself. I said, "Stop being a cheerful fraud to appease your mother. Tell her the truth."

"There's no such thing as a good day for me," Jordan admitted to her mom. "Every day I wake up to a nightmare."

Her mother started to cry and said, "How could that be?"

I thought of Harry Harlow's famous 1959 experiment with rhesus monkeys that showed how infant monkeys would cling more to a soft, surrogate mother that could not feed them than to a metal, milk-bearing one. They chose maternal soothing over food; that's how essential a mother's emotional warmth is to a baby. I wondered if Jordan's parents had given her everything except this kind of comforting affection.

As she kept speaking of her sadness and anger each week, I noticed that Jordan was coming to therapy looking less and less put together. Her hair wasn't as well combed, her clothes became more drab, her posture worsened until she was slumped over. Sometimes looking disheveled was a bad sign. With Jordan, I thought it was an improvement. I took it to mean that she was getting rid of her false front and was more willing to be who she really was with me.

When I asked if she had ever trusted anybody outside of herself, Jordan said that as a kid she loved a stuffed animal, a gray dolphin, that her mother had thrown away. After losing her beloved dolphin, she had a six-inch, blue pillow she'd embraced in times of stress. It was so old it had been recovered six times. I asked her to bring it in the next week. In that session, while talking about how disgusting her father said her tattoos were, Jordan started getting a migraine. I asked her to hold her pillow close and let herself cry. She wept. As she let her tears and her feelings flow, the migraine stopped. She was shocked. It was as if her inability to process her unhappiness had left everything bottled up and toxic inside her. I told her a saying she liked: "the opposite of DE-pression is EX-pression." By making more room for crying and despair, and trusting someone she could share it with, her migraines and leg shaking stopped.

After seeing Jordan for six months, other progress was touch and go. She reluctantly agreed to a moratorium on getting more body art and piercings, but I wasn't convinced she could stop. She broke up with her fiancé, started looking for a full-time job to add structure to her life, and continued therapy twice a week.

The biggest change happened when she returned to live at home, a move I encouraged. Jordan's parents stopped giving her an allowance so she couldn't spend any more of their money on tattoos, piercings, or drugs. Instead they took my suggestion to let Jordan turn her bedroom into a refuge and sanctuary. Jordan excitedly redecorated painting the walls and getting new pictures, lamps, and carpet that her parents paid for. She replaced the white, pink, and light pastels her mother picked out for dark blues and grays that suited and comforted her. Her father thought the extensive renovation was silly, but her mother grasped how important this was.

I've seen Jordan and her mother together several times. I'm trying to make sure Jordan is reassured that things have changed, that her living space is now more of a safe and soothing place, and that she is allowed to be herself and get real and doesn't have to fake it all the time. I encourage Jordan to continue her artwork. Some people with addictive personalities will always seek out different kinds of excitement and gravitate towards a variety of compulsive habits. I'm hoping that Jordan becomes obsessed with coloring in canvases instead of her skin.

HOW TO AVOID THE SUBSTANCE SHUFFLE

1. **GET HYPER-AWARE:** Closely monitor any changes or different activities you try. Get an outside opinion from a doctor, sponsor, relative, spouse, or friend you trust on the timing and frequency for each newfound idea or transition. Even seemingly healthy substitutes, like social life and exercise, need to be regulated with moderation, rules, and limitations.

2. **CONSUME CAREFULLY:** Watch everything you put in your mouth. Keep a journal and weigh yourself weekly or even daily if you are prone to food addictions. Even if you never had eating issues before, quitting an addiction can change your moods and metabolism. After quitting alcohol, you could easily become hooked on caffeine, the sugar or chemicals in soda, tea, coffee, or fruit juice (which may be healthy but is very high in calories). Even too much water (called water intoxication or overhydration) can be considered a poison when overconsumed, just like any other substance.

3. **MONEY MATTERS:** Keep a careful budget. Note any abrupt changes and have a plan to counter unusual spending. For example, if she plans to spend more than $500 for anything other than monthly bills, my coauthor, Susan, mentions it to me and her spouse before she makes the purchase. This is not to ask permission but rather to counterbalance her impulse to act on whims by debating whether it makes rational sense.

4. **GIVE SAFELY:** Watch any increases in gift giving, volunteering, and what you are donating to good causes and charity. Believe it or not, you can get carried away with the happy feeling you get from surprising someone with a special present, caretaking, or pledging a donation to a worthy cause. I call it "the Oprah syndrome." This can be a very sneaky addiction you can fall into without thinking. Without Oprah's income, it could lead to going broke or bankruptcy. Even if you can afford the time or money, your self-worth shouldn't get dependent on doing

good deeds, nor should you reach for constant "goodness" to fill in your emptiness.

5. **DON'T BET ON IT:** Even if you've never had a gambling problem, put limits on the amount you spend on lottery tickets, bingo, slot machines at casinos, and vacations. When I go to Las Vegas, I allow myself $1,000 to lose and make sure I don't take my credit cards, debit card, or checkbook. When my financial allotment is gone, it's time to go.

6. **CRUTCHES CAN BE DANGEROUS:** When you stop an addiction, do not allow yourself a free pass to use another habit as a crutch for long. Yes, after quitting alcohol, some people eat more sugar. But every time you bite into a donut, remember that using food could be repeating the vicious addiction cycle. If you gain twenty pounds, you might use it as an excuse to go back to drinking. The nicotine patch, gum, or inhaler are better than cigarettes for six months, but they can become unending addictions, too.

7. **BE HUMBLE AND HONEST:** I warn recovering addicts to remain as down to earth and close to the truth as possible. Any kind of falsification, magnification, or exaggeration comes from the same impulse to escape what is real and difficult.

8. **BE EMOTIVE:** Take time to vent all pent-up feelings of sadness, anger, confusion, or hurt. You are allowed to cry, scream, paint, or scrawl your rage into a notebook or computer. Repressed feelings will only pop up elsewhere, but worse.

9. **SWEAT IT OUT:** Sometimes a sport like boxing or soccer, where you hit or kick a ball or bag, can be a good outlet. Find a place where you can do it while crying or swearing if you need to.

10. **STAY SUPPORTED:** Keep going to recovery meetings, therapy sessions, regular appointments with doctors and sponsors, life coaching sessions, or health-oriented classes (meditation, yoga, nutrition). You might always need steady, healthy routines with people willing to offer advice and reality checks. There is a twelve-step debate about whether one can be fully recovered

versus being in recovery. I believe that an addict might be clean and sober for many years but you're never cured or completely rid of this impulse disorder. That's why when you quit a bad habit, you always have to be careful not to just switch to a different addiction.

CHAPTER 14

WHY AN ADDICT NEEDS RULES TO LIVE BY: OVEREXERCISING

"My marriage is a nightmare," Nadine told me during our first session in the winter of 2002. "My husband Harold is cold, critical, and abandoning. I feel so lost."

My patient, Nadine, was a pretty, five-foot-four, forty-four-year-old former lawyer originally from Saudi Arabia who had been referred to me through a colleague. She had short hair, wore no makeup, and had a no-nonsense air about her. She was poised, well spoken and had perfect posture, as if she had come from royalty, which, it turned out, she had. She spoke many languages, had a doctorate in art history, currently worked part-time at an uptown museum, and had two young children. That first day, she was in a sleeveless blouse and knee-length skirt that showed off noticeably muscular arms and legs. She wasn't ultraskinny; she weighed maybe 120 pounds. Her sculpted physique struck me as unusual for a middle-aged working mother, but I had no clue yet to the secrets her muscles were hiding.

When I asked about her past, Nadine casually chronicled growing up in a large, wealthy, Saudi Arabian-Muslim family, where her older brothers were treated like gods while she and her sister had been hit, starved, ignored, and chastised for such crimes as eating from the refrigerator or speaking out of turn. Nadine described her mother as aggressive, condescending, selfish, and obsessed with her jewels, houses, and social standing. In a political upheaval, they had lost their status and fled with their money to the United States when Nadine was a teenager. She excelled at school and married Harold, her first college boyfriend, when she was twenty, to escape her parents.

Of course there were big cultural differences between Manhattan and the Middle East. I knew pain from childhood abuse could lead to addictive behaviors. When I asked Nadine if she'd felt traumatized by such a harmful upbringing, she had little sympathy for herself.

"It wasn't that bad," she told me. "There are children starving in India who had it far worse than I did."

Nadine was obsessed with her failing marriage to Harold, a banker from a white, Southern-Lutheran clan. His background had alienated Nadine's parents and they had basically cut her off when she married. When Harold was getting his Ivy league MBA degree, Nadine fantasized about a sophisticated Manhattan life. But his business did not take off quickly and they wound up living in a Brooklyn Heights walkup. After his career flourished, they moved to Paris, where Harold confided that his dream was to be a father. Estranged from her own mother, Nadine had never wanted children, but to please Harold, she tried. Pregnancy did not happen easily. She quit her legal job and went through a decade and a half of infertility treatment, trying different doctors, medication, and corrective surgeries. After many rounds of IVF, she finally had a son and then a daughter whom she said she adored, both under five years old.

After the trouble she went through to give Harold a family, Nadine was outraged when he started cheating on her. When she learned he was having an affair with a childless woman half his age, Nadine angrily took the kids and moved back to Brooklyn Heights. "His coldness penetrates me and makes me feel how brutal and frozen life can be," she told me, in the precise, intense way she often spoke.

In that first session she threw in, "When I went running this morning . . ."

"So you're a runner?" I asked.

"Oh yes. I run every single day," she told me. "For three or four hours. I also bike, swim, and lift weights. If I miss a workout, I feel terrible."

Aha! That line was the tip off. Nadine did not drink, smoke, take drugs, or gamble. She said she had never been overweight and had always been active, but not extraordinarily so. My suspicion that exercise had become an addiction was confirmed when I asked Nadine to describe what happened when she missed a workout. She would get wildly depressed, frenzied, angry, and feel ready to explode. It sounded like the kind of withdrawal a smoker goes through without a cigarette. It was a confusing addiction to treat because unlike smoking, normal exercise has a positive side. Unlike adventure sports (like jumping out of planes or white-water rafting) there was rarely overt danger in running, cycling, or swimming.

Still, if left ignored and untreated, addictions always grow bigger. The disturbances they hide need to be aired, unpacked, and dealt with directly. Taken to extremes, benign-seeming habits like running, eating ice cream, or going to church functions can take over your life, to the detriment of everything else. That was the case with Nadine, who was literally running away from a world falling apart.

Yet exercise, healthy activity Nadine was valiantly using to help herself, had become an excessive cycle of self-medication. She bicycled everywhere and lifted weights daily. There was a gym in her apartment building, where running on the treadmill became her favorite hobby. She spoke of working out as if it were a drug that would solve all her problems, not realizing it was causing more. Nadine had no love in her life, didn't feel close to her kids, and wasn't thriving at work despite her enormous intelligence and extraordinary energy. The hours she ran directly interfered with developing other aspects of her life. After all, she wasn't an athlete in training for the Olympics or a professional dancer, where working out this much would be part of her job description. I wasn't sure if it was the endorphins she craved, the ritual, the escape, or a combination.

When I first suggested she was running too much, she argued. "But it's how I stay healthy, lean, and strong. How can something everybody says is good be bad for me?" she asked. I explained that too much of any substance or activity can be excessive and harmful. You can twist anything into a dangerous drug when it's main purpose is to avoid your feelings. The bottom line for Nadine: it wasn't working. She was still haunted by the unresolved issues that had followed her from her difficult childhood.

Her habit reminded me of the softball-playing hero of the David Shields novel *Dead Languages.* Any time anything went wrong, he went outside, grabbed a bat, and started swinging at a baseball because "we all go someplace to feel strong." Nadine wanted to feel stronger and regimented to combat feelings of weakness and chaos. Running cleansed her brain; she said after a run it was the only time she felt clean and soothed. Nadine's description of her marriage and upbringing showed why she needed so much soothing.

The compulsive exercising began two years earlier, as a reaction to her husband's infidelity. On the surface she hoped to make herself look younger and foil the aging process. She had a warped body image and desperately wanted to turn back time, fantasizing that a more fit physique would win back her spouse's affection. That was not happening. She was so upset about Harold's betrayal that she would get her kids off to school, then often go back to sleep. She managed to crawl out of bed only to work out and go to the museum once a week. During her first session, she admitted that she was so frustrated that she spanked her son and daughter.

It did not sound like she beat them or ever hit them with anything but her hand, yet as an abused child myself, any hitting of children rang alarm bells. Before discussing anything else, I gave her the number of a twenty-four-hour hotline for parents, which was completely anonymous. I insisted on implementing a new rule: when she felt angry, she had to pick up the phone, call the number and speak to someone immediately before touching her kids. As we made another session, she promised to do this if her temper flared. She seemed to be relieved by this rule.

During our second meeting, Nadine reported that she had become enraged when her daughter didn't clean her room, but instead of lifting her hand, which was her first impulse, she called the hotline and spoke to a woman who calmed her down. "You're angry and overwhelmed, you have every right to feel upset," the calm voice told her. "This feeling will pass." The hotline, which helped Nadine navigate troubled feelings, was entirely staffed by women. Perhaps it worked for her because it provided the voice of the nurturing mother she never had.

Her kids' demands for her attention rattled and overwhelmed Nadine. She was confused and drained by her husband's abandonment as well as her mother's constant interference, which exacerbated old feelings of rejection from which Nadine had never recovered. She was emotionally depleted. With no one caring for her, Nadine felt like she had nothing left to give her children.

I recommended she read *Healing the Shame That Binds You,* by recovery-counselor John Bradshaw. "Oh my god! He's writing about me!" Nadine later said, feeling a profound connection to Bradshaw's theories about the damaging effects of "toxic shame" rooted in early family dysfunction and abuse. She was starting to grasp how her painful past still controlled her. "My accomplishments should outweigh my low self-esteem, but nothing can fix it. I can't stop doubting myself. It's how I always feel. That's what my mother did to me." Nadine was relieved to feel she wasn't alone.

Her depression worsened as she and Harold divorced. I sent her to Dr. Sands, the psychopharmacologist with whom I often worked, who prescribed Prozac. The medication helped Nadine achieve more balance. It did not make her feel happy. I warn patients that antidepressants are never intended to make people feel good. They were invented to stop the agony of depression and take you off the edge so the right kind of human interaction could make a real difference.

Nadine began to view the women at the hotline, myself, Dr. Sands, and even Bradshaw as people offering her understanding and good advice. "I'm afraid I was becoming as cold and mean as my parents were to me," Nadine confided. After that realization, I was relieved that she completely stopped hitting her children. She was proud that she learned how to overcome her rage by talking it out; I encouraged that pride. She felt remorse for hitting her kids. "I need to undo the harm I've done, the way my parents never did for me," she said. Once I was confident that she had stopped punishing her kids physically (a rule about which I felt strongly) we moved on to other topics.

Nadine began taking her children to school, fixing up her house because she wanted her kids to have a nicer home, and cooking dinner. I encouraged her to ask them "Who is your favorite teacher? What's your worst subject at school?" and just listen to their answers with no judgments. When her son admitted he was having trouble reading, Nadine started reading fun books with her kids every night before bed. The school work of both her children improved greatly. I asked her to bring in pictures of herself as a child, and we worked on helping her develop empathy by remembering how she felt at her son's and daughter's ages. Nadine identified with their need for love, which her parents never gave her. By being more affectionate with her kids, she was healing herself.

By our second year of therapy, Nadine still overexercised. Along with running, lifting weights, and swimming, she rode her bicycle to our weekly sessions (ten miles back and forth from Brooklyn), leaving her bike in the hallway and blocking the bathroom. It was intrusive, as if she had no sense of community or family space. Because she had never gotten what she needed from her parents, I felt she still had a child's narcissistic personality. She had never been taken care of properly, so it was hard for her to put other's needs before her own.

I didn't demonize exercise since there was a band of fellow runners that Nadine enjoyed, and she needed friendship and a social life badly. If the choice was to sleep all day or to run for three hours, running was better. Emulating twelve-step programs that urge an addict to adopt a different code of behavior, we came up with new guidelines. Nadine agreed to work out less and make her priorities playing with her kids and logging in more hours at the museum. Not surprisingly, the changes made Nadine fearful and agitated.

She could not bear the normal aging process, worried that she would start sagging or lose her muscle tone. Yet she found it comforting to have a specific daily schedule to follow. This hour-by-hour plan, work, and therapy replaced the lost runs. Then something interesting happened. In her extra time at the museum, she met a coworker, an American divorcee with two kids of his own. As they dated, she was happy but cautious. "I really like him and he likes me, but in a relationship you can never tell. My children will always come first, you know," she said. Although she described her new beau as slim and attractive, it bothered her greatly that he did not exercise.

Nadine had solved what I considered to be her main problems—she stopped spanking her children, was dealing with her depression directly (with therapy, reading, identifying exactly what was hurting her), and was exercising less. Since there was an upside to working out, I never asked her to stop completely. But then a new difficulty arose. When he learned she had a boyfriend, her ex-husband, who had paid for 80 percent of Nadine and their children's bills, started withholding money and haggling over every dime. Her finances became a dilemma. She considering asking her parents for help, but said, "I fear they could try to take over my life the way my husband did." I encouraged Nadine to become financially independent.

Since she'd loved her involvement with her kids' schooling, she decided to launch her own education business, tutoring children with learning problems. It turned out to be extremely profitable, turning into an exciting new venture. While other members of her wealthy clan had to beg her tycoon father for funds, Nadine felt intense satisfaction supporting her family on her own. Her success was liberating.

As she replaced the overexercise with more satisfying pursuits, Nadine seemed more emotional and warmer. She laughed, loosened up, swore, and cried in front of me several times. Ultimately, she limited working out to a total of one hour a day, five days a week. Her running went from obsessive to what she called "rhythmic." It was a breakthrough when Nadine went three days in a row without exercising and did not feel upset or anxious. She was still in good shape but not as hard edged or muscular as when we first met. She looked better, softer, and more natural.

By letting in more people she could trust and moderating her extreme habit, Nadine was able to get much closer to her children. One day she came in thrilled that her son had done well in school. "I feel such joy for him, the joy I never felt when I was young," she told me, glowing with pride. "I want them to have the opposite childhood than I had so they won't grow up with the terror, sadness, and anxiety that I always have with me."

GUIDELINES FOR AN ADDICT

While codes, regulations, and strategies can be individualized for every different person and addiction, here are some overall rules that should be followed as a guideline for yourself or an addict in your world that you are worried about.

1. **DO NO HARM:** Any kind of bullying or physical abuse of children, partners, or parents crosses a line. I would recommend immediately calling the police, a school principal, social services, a therapist, or doctor for swift intervention. For any problems with children, call the Parent Hotline at (800) 840-6537. Remember you do not have to be alone.

2. **STAY LAWFUL:** All illegal activities are suspect. You can be arrested for buying a nickel bag of marijuana in the park or attempting to purchase liquor if you're underage. Any stealing, underage and unprotected sex with strangers, downloading child porno-

graphy, and selling drugs are cause to sound the alarm. If you don't want to alert the police, calling someone's spouse, parents, guardian, doctor, or principal to report these kinds of illegality can really help, especially when you find an appropriate authority figure who can offer wisdom and protection.

3. **ONLY DRIVE SOBER:** Operating a vehicle (car, motorcycle, boat, or plane) after you have had more than two drinks, smoked marijuana, or taken a mood-altering drug needs to be outlawed in every way imaginable, especially with passengers. Reminder: if anything bad happens, the driver can be incarcerated and charged with a crime.

4. **BE CAREFUL WHAT YOU CARRY:** Having illegal substances on you or transporting drugs through an airport is asking for serious trouble these days. When others are present, it puts them in the position of being arrested with you. If you find it impossible to be drug-free when you travel, a train or bus would be safer since there usually isn't national security checking everyone's bags and you are better off not being in the driver's seat. You are risking your life by taking or buying illegal drugs from strangers or in a foreign country.

5. **BE HOME SAFE:** Inviting drug dealers, prostitutes, or bookies into your residence when family members are there is completely unacceptable. It puts your relatives in what could be significant danger.

6. **BE DISARMING:** Drugs and weapons must be locked away and never left where anybody else might find and use them. A patient who lived alone left out pills that her dog wound up taking and it almost killed him. Now picture if that had been your child or grandchild.

7. **FOOD AND SHELTER FIRST:** You are never allowed to spend money earmarked for rent, food, day care, or education on your addiction. If possible, put funds in a separate account with limited access and pay bills with automatic banking that can't easily be changed and needs another's approval. Put as many blockades between you and your addiction as possible.

8. **WORDS COUNT:** Profanity and verbal abuse towards family members or underlings is not acceptable. It must be curtailed; its effects can be extremely harmful and long lasting.

9. **DYING FOR ATTENTION:** Any suicidal feelings or threats should be taken seriously. Immediate treatment with a doctor, counselor, or recovery professional is called for.

10. **LYING LOW:** Demanding that children or relatives keep substance issues a secret is damaging for everyone involved. If you are asking people to lie for you or someone is forcing you into silence, AA, Al-Anon, and Alateen meetings can be especially helpful to you or your family members trying to figure out how to cope with the dangers of a loved one's addiction.

CHAPTER 15

CHIPPING THE EDGE OFF NARCISSISM: PORNOGRAPHY

The New Yorker cartoonist Roz Chast recently started a line of narcissist greeting cards with such messages as "Wow! Your birthday's really close to mine. Isn't that amazing?" and "Speaking of Bon Voyage—guess where I'm going? France!"

Although the butt of many jokes, it's not fun or easy to be involved with a narcissist. This term refers to someone solipsistic, who has an often unconscious obsession with himself and his needs that shuts out any consideration for everybody else. The word is derived from the Greek mythological character Narcissus who looked into a pool, saw his own reflection in the waters, and fell in love with it, not realizing it was merely an image. He died because he was unable to let go of the obsession with his reflection. He literally drowned in it, as a modern-day narcissist so often "drowns" in his own self-regard.

In my experience, 99 percent of the addicts I've seen have strong narcissistic tendencies. That's because, as we've discussed, as a population they have felt so disappointed by their families and mates that they have basically given up on getting satisfaction and meaning from other humans and have turned to substances instead to feel soothed and taken care of. Everything has to serve them because they perceive that the right people didn't serve them in their childhood. Because of this early disappointment, others no longer really exist on their emotional radar screens, so they become narcissists by default. Those who are addicted think of themselves as profoundly alone in the world and only feel okay when they use cigarettes, alcohol, food, gambling, or other habits. How narcissistic an addict can be was brought to light by a fascinating addiction a patient of mine developed.

"I have a problem I don't want to discuss over the telephone," was the first message left by Phillip, an actor referred to me by another patient in March of 2001. His voice was filled with guilt, embarrassment, and shame—good signs. The fact that he already acknowledged he had a problem that bothered him seemed to me a better starting point than the denial I sometimes heard from patients who called for an appointment.

"Is it possible to be addicted to porn?" Philip asked when I met him.

"Yes, without a doubt." I explained it was possible to be addicted to any substance or activity.

Phillip was a handsome, forty-seven-year-old, single guy who lived in Williambsurg. He was six foot two, with big shoulders and curly black hair that fell over his eyes. He was wearing blue jeans, an un-tucked work shirt, and sneakers, a little disheveled, like you might expect a Brooklyn actor to look. He had a friendly, charming manner, relaxed but inherently anxious.

While researching a role about a porn star a year before, he started frequenting a certain porn page. It was a design-your-own-lover website where you could plug in specific features—blond hair, big breasts—and form a realistic-looking, perfect partner that looked like a *Playboy* centerfold. Phillip would do this and masturbate many times a day to the image he had created. His ejaculations became minimal and painful, until he was physically exhausted.

As he spoke about it, I had a strong sense that he was developing serious emotional connections with these perfectly formed cyber women and these relationships had a manic, real, cure-everything-that-bothers-you quality. He could not stay away from them, nor could he identify the needs in him that they satisfied. He knew that he had crossed the line between entertainment and obsession and now his fetish had an irresistible, almost hallucinatory draw he could not resist. It was as if he was in the middle of an ecstatic love affair with the female of his dreams. He could not stop. He was currently visiting his fantasy girlfriends constantly, the way others checked email or Facebook. Although Phillip was paid residuals for national commercials in which he'd appeared, he was currently working as an acting coach. His penchant for pornography was sidetracking him from other goals like getting a starring movie or theater role, affording an apartment in Manhattan, and finding a real sex partner, girlfriend, or wife.

Sometimes the hallmark of an addiction is not the failures and horrors it brings into your life, but instead the missed opportunities that happen as a result of the time and attention spent on satisfying the addiction. Getting married, having children, relating to one's spouse or child, or achieving the next level of success in one's career all get put on the back burner so that the craving for the addiction can be satisfied. A compulsion like this can be time consuming and expensive and often takes top priority in an addict's life.

There appeared to be a distinct pattern in Phillip's romances with actual women. He dated around a lot, until he would meet somebody and fall head over heels too quickly—within a few weeks. He would remain infatuated and monogamous for about two months. He would dote on his girlfriend and act emotionally generous, in a way that females found compelling. His girlfriends would fall for this and think they were in love with him. Then he would notice something wrong with his partner—her brown hair was too dark, her chin was too short, she had a tiny mole on her cheek. Suddenly he could not look at anything else but her blemish. The blemish told a story that filled his entire consciousness: this is not the perfect woman. Soon he was no longer interested in the flawed human being he had been dating and he abandoned her. Then he would meet another woman to idealize. She, too, would fail him, and the pattern continued with no end in sight.

As addictions go, this one seemed to me closest to a reliance on nicotine. Phillip could access the porn website twenty-four hours a day, in the same way a pack-a-day smoker always carries around cigarettes in his or her pocket or purse. Viewing these sexual images took Phillip out of reality as often as twenty times a day, stimulating him for a short period of time, satisfying his longing for oneness and calm even though it left him ultimately alone, drained, and unsatisfied. He had nothing in his life to relieve the loneliness except turning on the computer and returning to the vicious cycle of feeling fake love and then finding himself utterly empty.

Phillip had gone to Yale Drama School, which did not surprise me, since he was very intelligent and well spoken. He was the middle of three children, the second son from a middle-class, nonpracticing, wealthy, Presbyterian family in Oregon. Both his older brother and younger sister were married with children and living on the West Coast. He called himself the black sheep of the family. His parents divorced when he was fifteen years old. He described his mother as loving but passive. Like the typical middle child, he seemed to have gotten somewhat lost in the family. Although he was being supported by his father, a businessman, he was angry with him and called him selfish and self-centered. Since his parents divorced, his father had also gone through innumerable girlfriends looking for the ideal mate who met all the criteria of his unrealistic fantasies.

"I'm afraid I'm becoming my dad," he said. "And I hate my dad."

Indeed, his immature patterns with women mirrored his father's in many ways. I saw Phillip's issues as having characteristics that were quite typical of male, narcissistic patients I'd seen. He was looking for someone who he would never find. He was searching for dream lovers based on his own needs that had nothing to do with who the women really were. I had seen this dynamic many times and told Phillip there was only one radical strategy I knew that could effectively break through this wall and change his self-defeating pattern. When it came to romantic relationships, his happiness and needs were no longer to be considered relevant. If he focused on his own needs, whatever he did with another human being would be dominated by himself. Any chance for true love would be trumped by his own self-centered psychology. The only thing to be considered important was his ability to bring happiness to the woman in his life, something he had never done before.

I suggested this because, in my experience, a narcissistic man will never be able to find exactly what he wants in a woman; therefore, a woman will never make him happy. He had to try something new, to stop focusing on his own bottomless desires and care more about someone else instead.

"But what about my needs?" he asked.

"You have been trying to satisfy yourself for years and it has never worked. So you don't matter anymore," I told him. "Here's the secret: you will ultimately derive happiness from bringing love and satisfaction to somebody else and from that person loving you fully and completely in response to your emotional generosity. But don't tell yourself that because then you will be doing it for all the wrong reasons. The point is to put the other person at the center of your radar screen and move yourself to the side, to concern yourself with somebody else's desires, letting go of your own."

I suggested he read Freud's writing on narcissism and Alice Miller's *Drama of the Gifted Child,* and come to see me once a week. This was difficult for him financially, but he agreed. I asked how long he thought he could survive without turning to the pornography. He said one week, but he made it for only two days. Without it, he felt bored, depressed, and agitated, as if he didn't know what to do with himself. He felt horribly alone. With external addictions like gambling and pornography, which are not literally in your blood stream (like cigarettes, cocaine, and alcohol), patients do not have physical withdrawal symptoms. They do not shake or sweat the way addicts often do when detoxing. They go straight to the feelings of gloom, emptiness, and depression—the very emotions their addictions were meant to help them escape.

In Phillip's case I thought his sadness was rooted in disappointment early in his life. Because of my own fascination with maternal angst, I saw the quest to find the perfect "other" as the search for the ideal mother that one never had. I explained my theory to Phillip (based on Freud, Melanie Klein, Bion, and other psychoanalysts I admired) that infants and their mothers were literally merged as one in the womb. After birth, an infant experienced a good mother as an extension of himself. If you did not fully get your mother's attention and affection before the age of five, the window to that kind of early love was forever closed. It was pointless to think otherwise, since no human woman could ever live up to the idealized maternal image that one had never experienced as a young child. He had to stop looking for the woman who would adore and take care of the three-year-old Phillip because that woman did not exist anywhere but in his fantasy.

Over the next month, he cut down on the amount of times he would visit the pornography website. It was very hard for him. Along with seeing me, he began going to twelve-step meetings for sex addicts twice a week. Although they were not specifically for pornography, the interactions with others who had similar sexual issues seemed to help him. After five months of seeing me, in August he began dating a new woman named Fiona. She was pretty and smart, a college professor. He fell in love with her too fast, following his usual pattern.

After two months, he found the blemish. He learned that she had overcome bipolar disorder and had to take medication. It greatly bothered him and we discussed it at length. Phillip realized that he was overreacting. After all, this bipolar individual was also a college professor who had very impressively conquered all the obstacles to find success in her field. Still, in Phillip's distorted realm, Ms. Right had turned into Ms. Flawed and he wanted to flee.

"You're turning into your father," I said. "That's exactly the kind of thing your father would do. He would run away."

"I'm not my dad," he argued with me, and with himself.

His priority became fixing his relationship with Fiona. He concentrated on making her happy in small ways: letting her choose the movie, restaurant, or play they were going to and hanging out with her friends instead of his. We talked about his mixed emotions weekly, discussing why "feelings misinform," and how addicts' emotions always lead them back to their bad habits. He had to stop relying on how he felt and start living his life according to a set of rational rules, guidelines, and principles that were not connected to how he felt.

After two years, Phillip's longest relationship, he brought Fiona into therapy with him. She was humble, modest, calm—a substantial person whom I liked. Although he completely stopped going to the pornography website, Phillip nevertheless felt powerful cravings. While he never went back to porn, he wound up breaking up with Fiona, sure that a more perfect girl was somewhere out there for him. As far as I know, he has yet to find her.

In some ways I consider myself to have traits of a recovering narcissist. I realize you are never fully recovered and have to stay vigilant in order to not lose sight of the needs and desires of other people you care about. I have been able to undercut my own narcissistic tendencies by remaining in a profession where I help people. I also make a conscious decision to offer sliding scales at my institute, volunteered to help people recover at Ground Zero after 9/11, and contribute to a foundation that helps children who have cancer and a charity that helps people who have been traumatized but can't afford medical and psychiatric treatment.

After Susan, a childless workaholic, quit her addictions by refocusing her passion on her career, she worried that she was spending too much of her time and energy chasing after bylines and checks. While the fame game was fun, it was also exacerbating her myopic and self-involved tendencies.

At the time, she was teaching one journalism class at night, which made her feel like she was giving back. Together we worked out a strategy where she cut down on freelancing and increased her course load to three nights a week. She also began teaching in a volunteer program at a local soup kitchen. Interestingly, she felt all the good karma she amassed from helping others wound up helping her sell more books, including one about that soup-kitchen program.

Addiction recovery often forces you to be very self-involved and self-protective for awhile, which is healthy. But if you fear your narcissism might be hindering your relationships or career long term and don't want to lead a selfish life, here are some ways you can consciously ensure a better balance.

1. **PAY IT UP:** When you receive payment or a monetary gift you don't need for paying bills, donate a part of it—even 5 percent—to a good cause. Anytime she earns over $1000, Susan first writes a check to charity, then she buys herself a present of the same amount. The rest goes directly into the bank to pay her bills.

2. **BE A TEAM PLAYER:** When Susan does a group reading or panel, she makes a point to include other authors and to buy the books of everybody there, often leaving with as many as seven or eight signed books. Since she wants people to go to her many readings and events, she makes it a rule to show up to other literary events she's invited to at least once a week, as a matter of practice, and always buys the book to honor the featured author. (Even if it's a competitor who didn't buy hers!)

3. **VOLUNTEER YOUR TIME:** Be a mentor, a big brother or sister, deliver food to homebound elderly, or serve meals at a food pantry. Even two hours a week can make a difference to other people, and to yourself, and costs only time and kindness. Pick a charity that has deep meaning for you. If someone you love had breast cancer, do the Breast Cancer Awareness walk. If you love animals, give time to a pet shelter.

4. **RECONSIDER YOUR FIELD:** Consider nonprofit jobs that will increase your compassion for others. One patient of mine left a

high-pressure technology job to work with a women's welfare agency all over the globe and has found her calling.

5. **PART-TIME JOB:** Teaching an evening class, part-time coaching, fund-raising, tutoring, or mentoring might offer less pay but much more satisfaction.

6. **OFFER TLC TO FRIENDS OR RELATIVES IN NEED:** Pledge to make one extra phone call a week to an elderly relative who is lonely. Babysit or do a play-date for a working mother who never gets any time on her own.

7. **ASK QUESTIONS:** Instead of launching into stories about your life or relationships or career, make a point to ask people about themselves first. Whether it's a date, business meeting, social gathering, or meal with a family member or friend, suppress your urge to share your usual monologue until the other person has spoken or given his or her opinion.

8. **PRESENT TENSE:** If somebody has helped you or been especially kind, return his or her kindness with a small present or thank-you card or treating for a special meal. Susan told me of the time she asked an editor who had given her a great assignment to lunch. When the bill came, she insisted on treating. The editor said "In twenty years on the job, no writer has ever taken me to lunch before." Although $100 was a lot for her to pay for lunch at that point, she felt it was only fair. This same editor ended up assigning her a monthly book column, adding $12,000 to her annual salary the next year. Good deeds and kindness always do come around; that's the concept of good karma.

9. **EXPAND YOUR GUEST LIST:** If you are throwing a party, dinner, or event and have extra room, don't only include the cool cats who make you look good and get invited everywhere. Be sure to invite some single, older, widowed, divorced, or lonely friends or acquaintances who might not have a place to go and will really appreciate a special soiree.

10. **START WITH A COMPLIMENT:** Instead of starting a conversation by sharing what's going on with you, find something you like

about the person you're with and begin with that, even if it's minor. When your mate or relative comes home at night say "Great jacket" or "I like your haircut" or "your smile is so winning." Make a point of doing this at business meetings, parties, and family gatherings.

11. **LET SOMEONE ELSE TAKE THE LEAD:** Even though you really want Chinese food, compromise if your friend prefers Italian. When you'd rather watch *Mad Men* DVDs, let your child pick *Barney*. Yes, you'd prefer a shoot-em-up movie, but if your mate wants to see a weepy movie, be generous and give it a shot. Sometimes it's a good exercise to put someone else's needs before your own and the amount of love you engender will wind up benefiting you the most.

12. **GIVE YOUR UNDIVIDED ATTENTION:** When you come home to your parents, spouse, children, roommates, or friends, make a point to turn off your TV, computer, iPhone, iPad, iPod, and all other electronic equipment and really be there. I remember once when she was seven, my daughter put her hand on my busy Blackberry and said, "Shhh. Just be with me and watch me play." As I turned it off and watched her play, I realized that simply being with another person in his or her space and putting my own needs aside could open a door to an intimacy I had never experienced before.

CHAPTER 16

SWITCH TO HEALTHY SUBSTITUTES: SURVIVING BULIMIA & ALCOHOLISM

"I'd like an appointment," Lilly told my answering machine in November 1999. She left only her name and number. Her message was cryptic and minimal, as if she doled out words crumb by crumb. She seemed like someone who wanted to let as little in and as little out as possible. Everything was contained and under wraps. When I called back, Lilly said that her mother had heard about my reputation and mentioned she had food issues she wouldn't discuss on the phone. I referred her to Harriet, a psychologist at my institute who specialized in eating problems.

"Why not you?" Lilly wanted to know.

"Harriet can work with you on sliding scale," I said.

"Don't you see patients with eating disorders?" she asked.

I did indeed treat patients for problems with overeating, dieting, anorexia, bulimia, binging, and overexercising. On the surface, those with eating disorders appeared different than drug addicts or alcoholics, yet I found that they fit the overall pattern of addiction and recovery. In fact, because food was so easily available, cheap, offered so many choices, and it was necessary to eat to live, food was one of the most common substances abused. There were very few people I knew who did not have trouble or confusion about their weight and daily food intake. Consequently, food disorders were among the most difficult to treat. Recovering alcoholics stayed off drink, cocaine addicts gave up coke forever, and smokers kicked the habit in an all-or-nothing way. It was always easier to stop something 100 percent than to do it moderately, but no patient could simply stop eating.

"Why would paying your fee be an issue for me?" Lilly asked, in a challenging, disdainful voice.

I had mistakenly assumed, because Lilly sounded young and tentative on the phone, was female, and had eating issues, that she was a college girl with financial limitations. I was charging $200 a session for new patients at that point, while I let less experienced therapists who were trained at The Village Institute charge between $50 and $175, depending on what a patient could afford. I told Lilly my fee.

"That's fine," she snapped. "I will see only you and not anybody else."

Her voice sounded demanding, bossy, and rigid, as if she was saying, "It's my way or the highway." That was the brick wall that I would have to break through. Before I had even met her or knew what her exact problem was, Lilly presented a paradox. She was saying, in essence, "I don't want anybody but you," yet at the same time, she was not going to let me in except on her own terms.

It was my belief that any addict who insists on remaining totally in control cannot be helped. An essential step for any addiction patient is to give up control and let another person become a significant influence. (This mirrors AA's concept of the "higher power" and most treatment centers' strict rules.) I have found that addicts as a group have had such bad experiences with parents and loved ones that they basically replace people with substances, renouncing human dependency. You can be dependent on a substance while at the same time retaining the illusion of total control. That illusion had to be relinquished in order to break the addiction. The need for other people had to be made conscious.

Lilly, who said she had a flexible schedule, came to see me two days later. She was nineteen, with long brown hair, tall, about five foot nine. She was very thin. I guessed she weighed 110 pounds or less. She looked at least twenty-five pounds underweight. At first she appeared to have the taut, skeletal look of a Holocaust survivor, yet from another angle she looked quite beautiful. She was wearing blue jeans and an untucked, long-sleeved T-shirt, casual but neat. I thought she was very poised and strong for somebody so stick thin; she did not give off any semblance of weakness or frailty.

I happened to glance down at her feet and noticed she was wearing sandals with no socks, even though it was November and thirty-five degrees outside. Not being dressed appropriately for the season suggested that she did not feel the impact that the natural world had on her body. I surmised that she did not experience cold or hot or pain like others did. She lived so much inside her own head that she was able to simply ignore the weather and the effect that external stimuli had on her.

Lilly was from an Upper East Side, wealthy, nonpracticing, Presbyterian family of high-society bankers, the same milieu in which I'd grown up. She was not working and lived alone in an expensive uptown apartment paid for without question or supervision by her family. She was not a full-time college student either, which explained her loose schedule. She was taking one philosophy class but was more interested in white-water rafting and parasailing. She was one of three siblings, with one sister and a brother. She said that her brother, who was five years older, had molested her several times when she was young. She now revealed that the eating problem she had referred to on the phone was bulimia, technically called hyperphagia. She had been making herself throw up as often as ten times a day since she was fourteen. She was so good at it she did not even have to stick her finger down her throat. She could contract her stomach muscles according to a certain pattern and regurgitate at will.

There was an obvious link to her brother molesting her and Lilly becoming bulimic. By refusing to not keep any food down and staying so thin, her body looked like a boy's. She had very small breasts and hips. I guessed she wanted to repress the most obvious signs of female sexuality. After her brother's betrayal, she told her parents, who did not want to even hear of such things happening in their family. They did not believe her or do anything about what had happened. Lilly's reaction was to shut up, shut down, and throw up. She escaped to prep school at fourteen and avoided being home after that. She felt nothing good could ever come from connections with men. She took a closed-off, antidependent approach ("I don't need anything from anybody") to protect herself.

"I have been in therapy before and I can see right through every therapist," she warned me at our first session. "If the best you can do is to try to cure my bulimia, it won't work, because psychologists are very stupid people. I do not intend to waste a lot of time and money, as I have in the past, making you feel good about yourself."

It was a powerful statement. I felt like I was in the middle of a chess game with a worthy opponent. This was going to be a power struggle which I thought Lilly needed me to win. If I was not strong enough, I would be just one of the many shrinks who had failed her. She would have no use for me and would not get the help she so desperately needed.

"You have no right to speak to me in that haughty tone of voice and tell me how stupid therapists are," I told her, correct as she might have been. At that same session, when she misused a word, I also pointed out the right way to say it, adding, "Nobody will ever respect you if you abuse the English language. You should consider going back to school as well as being back to therapy." I was responding to her sarcasm, arrogance, and condescension in kind. If she was going to verbally cut me with a sharp edge, I would cut her back just as much so that the playing field was level and that she did not have the upper hand.

"Okay, then," she nodded. "Obviously you're different than the therapists I've met before." She smiled, looking relieved that I was not intimidated by her.

At the beginning I was speaking to Lilly in the manner of a stern parent, as I often did, knowing firsthand that people who did not grow up with effective authority figures crave that kind of strong parental guidance. I was taken aback the next session when out of the blue she said, "Well, now, do you want to tell me about your absent mother?"

Where did that come from? I wondered. "Apparently you know what that's like," I said, turning it back to her.

"You mean you can't talk about the violence?" she asked, contentious and hostile, yet perceptive enough to unnerve me.

"I don't want to talk about my mother yet," I said, trying to establish our priorities and boundaries. "And it's rude to use your x-ray vision when there are things I am not ready to share with you. You need to learn better manners."

"Why?"

"If you are not respectful in a discussion with someone older, who has every intention of being on your side, then you are going to lose the best ally you ever had. That would be rather stupid on your part."

"Between you and your mother, there was only room for one to survive. That's why you learned to fight so hard and be strong," she told me. "But inside I know that your biggest problem is letting someone else take care of you."

"So that makes two of us," I said.

Her brain and pure, primitive powers of intuition were so sharp that it almost made me uncomfortable. Sometimes I thought Lilly's ambition in therapy was to outshrink me. I later decided that she must have realized the only way I could so deeply empathize with her pain was if I had survived a similarly degrading kind of family neglect and abuse myself. Since she was afraid of any kind of intimacy, I took it as a good sign that she felt safe enough to let me know she knew, even indirectly.

Out of all the patients I had ever treated, it was odd that I identified so much with a nineteen-year-old, female bulimic. From very early in her treatment, I saw my younger self in her. Maybe we understood each other because we had so much in common. We had both grown up in the same rich, Upper East Side neighborhood feeling lost and neglected. We both turned against food, albeit in very different ways.

When I was a teenager, I, too, was skinny because I refused to eat enough. My mother was a gourmet cook who made food spicy and tangy. I wanted comfort food. Throughout my childhood, food was a source of pain for me. Although I never threw up, by my teenage years, I felt that the cigarette I smoked after dinner was the best part of any meal. Often I picked at my plate while craving the sensation of smoking later. I felt no satisfaction from the food. The cigarette was what would satisfy and calm me. It took away the discomfort of my mother's food, and subsequently of all meals, in a way that reminded me of Lilly's bulimia. She'd once described it as a numbing process, in the way that an alcoholic felt more sedated after a few martinis. Both my smoking and her bulimia served to change an internal state, to maintain emotional equilibrium, so both fit the definition of an addiction.

In the next few months, I learned more about Lilly's illness. It had been going on steadily for five years and was so extreme that she had been an inpatient in hospitals many times. Each time she was hospitalized, she would run away. Everybody—her parents, sibling, doctors, and high school teachers—knew about her eating disorder. She had been on antidepressants and numerous other medications, none of which were helping her.

I asked more about Lilly's background. Neither of her siblings had eating disorders or addictions. Her sister was gay and her brother, who had molested her, was now engaged. Lilly was the only one currently living in Manhattan. She was also the only one whom her brother had touched inappropriately. I encouraged her to speak to him about it. "Why don't you write him a letter, asking if he remembers that it happened?" I suggested, so she wouldn't be the only one in the world stuck with the uncorroborated memory. She refused. Her parents knew something had happened but did not want to know more, and they refused to talk about it with Lilly. They moved to Colorado and the only time the whole family was together was once a year, for Christmas. After hearing the whole story, I recommended she avoid her family as much as possible since when she was around them she felt profoundly unsafe and unprotected.

Lilly soon mentioned she was drinking a lot of wine, which led her to get into bad situations with men. She did not seem like an alcoholic or a sex addict, more like a lost little girl susceptible to any guy who paid attention to her. One time she met an older photographer on the street who said, "You're beautiful. I can make you a star." She got caught up in the fantasy that this man might be powerful enough to make her a famous model. She planned on going to California with him the day after they'd met until I intervened, even suggesting that I might call her parents if she left the state with him. After that she decided to see me twice a week, paid for by her family. Clearly her decision-making process was impaired, but she was starting to trust my judgment. The biggest problem in Lilly's treatment was that I was her only core pillar. Outside of therapy she had no structure in her life and no parental guidance. Once again I played that role.

"I'm afraid you'll lose yourself in a dangerous situation and alcohol will push you over the edge," I told her.

After discussing her drinking for several months, she was able to give it up. I was not sure which was harder: for Lilly to stop drinking as an escape or crutch, or for her to collaborate with me, or anyone, about major decisions in her life.

Lilly enrolled in a few more classes and worked part-time at a local bookstore, replacing her dangerous obsessions with something healthier, more meaningful, and stable. She finally stopped throwing up completely. She gained a little weight and I began to speak with her about enrolling in school full-time.

Part of her therapy involved accounting for how she spent all of her hours. I wanted to know what Lilly was doing every day, from when she woke up in the morning until she went to sleep. Too much freedom offers too many choices that an addict cannot handle. I asked her to write down her daily plans and print them out for me. I wanted her to be responsible, to report back to me, explain, and justify her whereabouts. I asked her to leave phone messages on my machine three times a day to tell me how she was doing with food and whether she threw up or not. I often encourage an addict to create an hour by hour plan of what he or she has to do and where he or she needs to be. Then I push the patient to commit to the plan he or she has devised. This usually involves school, work, a healthy kind (and amount) of exercise, seeing family or friends, or twelve-step meetings, which help to cut down on substance abuse.

Eventually, after much coercing and discussion, Lilly complied. She was accountable, both to me and to her schedule. She was ambivalent about surrendering to it, hating to rely on somebody else.

When it came time for her brother's wedding, Lilly's parents told her she had to be there. She decided to show up, fearing they would punish her by cutting her off financially if she didn't. Since she'd made the decision to go, I didn't argue. Instead I helped to prepare her. First, we figured out she could maintain better distance by staying at a hotel on her own. She promised not to drink any alcohol, do drugs, have sex with anyone, or throw up while she was there. At the reception she made a point of mingling more with strangers than relatives. I told her to phone me in case of emergency or leave messages on my machine as often as she needed to. She didn't. She reported the experience was numbing and "weird" but was over soon and not unbearable.

Not long after that, when Lilly's father was in New York, he called me for a consultation and came in. He was a musician, and an alcoholic. He didn't seem like a bad person, just weak. I was upset with him and frustrated; I felt like telling him he needed to work harder to take care of his daughter. But I couldn't undo the past and didn't want to alienate him for fear it could hurt Lilly. So I calmly stressed the importance of him continuing to pay for her rent, her medical needs, her college degree, and her therapy.

Then Lilly's mother called and came in. She was a teacher. (Although they lived off family money, they did not wear any of the usual trappings of wealth.) She was attractive, on the thin side, and apparently had had an eating disorder once herself. She seemed guilty and helpless. She wound up coming in for ten sessions. While Lilly and her father were estranged, Lilly was emotionally enmeshed with her mother as well as antagonistic towards her. Theirs was not a love/hate relationship; I would call it need/hate. So, unfortunately, she couldn't really be a core pillar. Although I felt like bluntly bringing up the abuse in Lilly's past, I didn't want to exacerbate an already fraught, dysfunctional situation and make it worse for Lilly. I subtly suggested Lilly's mother get together with her daughter one-on-one to bring up the bad things that happened to Lilly in the past, and listen to what she had to say without responding at all or getting defensive. She could call me if she had any questions or needed to argue or deny or defend herself.

I hoped Lilly's trust in me would provide a foundation that would allow her to find other core pillars. Although she refused to go to any recovery groups, she applied to a four-year college program to get her undergraduate degree.

Lilly had a few relapses with bulimia, but luckily she kept coming to therapy and continued working at her part-time job. At twenty-four, she was very pleased to be accepted to a good university. She enrolled full-time and that soon became her new life, her preoccupation, and her (healthier) substitute family. She decided to major in philosophy. I was also a philosophy major in college, so we had many discussions on the subject. She loved pointing out when my statements were formally illogical.

PLACES TO LOOK FOR HEALTHIER SUBSTITUTES

I know I keep repeating similar recommendations, but these are the arenas that offer the best choices for people who are ready to get clean and reinspired.

1. School programs
2. Work you enjoy
3. Charity/volunteering opportunities
4. Social organizations
5. Recovery meetings
6. One-on-one therapy or counseling sessions
7. Moderate exercise (alone or with trainers or sports teams)
8. Weekly religious services or activities
9. Artistic outlets (whether it's going to plays, movies, dance recitals, readings, or getting involved in productions yourself)
10. Spending times with friends you trust, especially ones who are sympathetic to your struggles

THE REALITIES OF RELAPSE: CRACK & CRIME

"My eighteen-year-old son Lance is in trouble. He's involved with drugs and really needs your help," was the message I received the summer of 1989 from Mrs. T., Lance's mother, who wanted me to treat her rebellious teenager. I asked her if Lance would call me himself. If a patient is dragged in by his mom or dad, I get associated with the enemy camp. I wanted to be the kid's ally, even if that meant keeping distance between myself and the referring parent. The next day I took a phone call from Lance, who said, "Hey, doc, my mom said to call for an appointment. When can I see ya?" His language was informal, with an I-don't-give-a-damn-what-you-think-of-me tone.

"Your mom wants to come in with you the first time. Why don't we see what's on her mind?" I said. I did not want to meet with his mother alone first, which might make Lance paranoid about what she revealed. But I also did not want to alienate the person who would be paying for his treatment and thus making help possible.

"Fine with me. Whatever you want, man," he said. "I don't really care."

I assumed Lance was drinking, smoking weed, sniffing cocaine, or dropping acid like other young patients coming to my Long Island office at that point. I was surprised to learn it was much more serious—he had been arrested twice for possession of cocaine and marijuana. Worse, he had been violent and had attacked the police officer who had arrested him.

Mrs. T. was in her forties, attractive, nicely dressed in a pants suit, well groomed, and neat. She was from old money, of Scandinavian descent, and they belonged to an Episcopal church. Lance was five foot seven, with shoulder-length blond hair. He wore dirty khakis, a T-shirt, and sneakers. He could have been good looking but made no effort. He might have been athletic at one point but now his expression was tired, as if he had been through too much. He seemed like a middle-aged teenager.

"Let your mother talk first," I told Lance. "If you want to interrupt, just bite your tongue. You'll get your chance when your mother leaves."

Normally teenagers do not want to talk to therapists. I would worry about a kid who wanted to open up to me right away, which would suggest the patient was desperate, dealing with serious abuse at home, and had nobody at all in his or her life, yet once I shut kids up, teens rebel against my gag order and want to talk. Lance tried to interrupt a few times, but I shut him down, saying, "Not yet. You'll get your turn." I knew I was frustrating him and that he'd be eager to get his side out when his mother left.

Mrs. T. said that Lance was a straight-A student teachers had once called "brilliant," albeit an out-of-the-box thinker. He had become an angry misfit who skipped school and came home at all hours of the morning. "We can't control him anymore," she lamented. Her husband, a successful businessman, couldn't relate to Lance's fringe music and anarchist politics and had checked out emotionally.

When parents of young addicts feel powerless, I suggest getting more involved, not less. Call teachers and principals every day to make sure your kid is going to class. Don't give him an allowance he could use to buy drugs. Instead of handing over car keys, drive him to school yourself. Hell, if your kid is doing drugs in your home, remove the door to his bedroom. If he screams, "I deserve privacy," tell him that his door will be returned when he abides by the laws—of the land and your house. When I learned my own son was dabbling with alcohol and drugs in college, I flew to his school the day I found out. I didn't care that some people felt it was entirely normal for a kid his age to experiment and that I was overreacting. I stopped trouble in its tracks, before it turned into something more serious. Of course I know that harsh tactics don't always work or help quickly, yet they may have made a difference when Lance began getting high at thirteen.

Mrs. T. told me that they had bailed Lance out twice with an expensive lawyer, using connections with the DA's office to get the charges removed from his record.

"Why did you do that?" I asked her.

"Well, we couldn't have him go to jail, could we?" she asked me.

"Why not?"

She was worried, yet seemed ineffectual and cloaked in denial. I sometimes feared that relatives of addicts worried more about their status, social embarrassment, and what the neighbors think than how to actually help their disturbed child.

"He could get hurt or killed in jail," she said.

"I know you want to be good parents, but I don't agree with the way you are dealing with your son," I told her. I explained that paying for lawyers and therapy showed they cared, but writing checks is never enough to solve an addict's problems. Parents feel that doing this helps them dodge a bullet when, in actuality, they are only postponing inevitable explosions that will come later. Or making far more harm possible than what could happen if their son was in jail.

After I said, "I think Lance has been getting off too easy," Lance snorted, rolling his eyes. This slacker was not only sloppy, angry, and derisive, he was lawless, not even pretending to show respect for me, his mother, or the police officers who had arrested him. This patient was proving to be much more challenging than I'd thought.

By the time I asked his mother to leave, Lance looked ready to talk.

"So, let's hear the real story now," I said. "I never believe what parents tell me because they don't often know what's going on in their kid's mind."

"Where do you want me to start, man?" he asked.

"Start with the worst."

"You really want the worst?" he asked, now looking uptight, anxious, and paranoid.

"Secrets cause people agony," I said. "It's usually a relief to get them out in the open."

"Two crack dealers are after me because I took some stuff to sell. I got stoned, then got robbed," he said. "They won't believe me. They're going to get me, man. I'm dead."

At this stage of my practice, I had rarely seen a middle-class suburban kid with these problems. Was he actually a crack dealer in fear for his life? I didn't know if he was lying or exaggerating.

"These guys really want to murder you?" I asked.

"For real. If these guys catch up to me, maybe they won't kill me," Lance said. "But you'll be visiting me in the hospital, man. That's for sure."

I believe the feelings that patients induce in me are a good measure of the truth. I knew Lance was not lying because I felt afraid for him. When I learned the death threats were over $500 and Lance had the money, I advised him to be practical and pay off the dealers right away to get rid of the problem.

Asking about his drug history, Lance said he had not only been using pot and cocaine since he was thirteen, but he was also dealing himself. Furthermore, he was selling crack, which he'd been freebasing since he was sixteen. Seeing a teenager who freebased crack three times a week shook me.

The National Institute on Drug Abuse lists side effects of crack as intestinal damage, nerve damage, seizures, constricted blood vessels, insomnia, cardiac arrest, paranoia, paranoid psychosis, hallucinations, and violent behavior extreme enough to sometimes even cause suicide and murder. A former patient told me that boiling cocaine down and smoking it, the way Lance did, created an unparalleled, dangerous, addictive high that lasted five or six hours. It offered such a potent, euphoric buzz that Lance later sniffed heroin to chase it and calm down. Being stoned on this drug was so good, I heard, every other sensation felt dull and stupid in comparison.

I recalled a prominent restauranteur I knew who confided in me that he had tried every drug around—pot, LSD, cocaine, mushrooms, speed, heroin, and pills. "The only one I'd never do again is crack," he told me. "Because if I ever took it again, I would never stop. It was that good. It was like being in God's right hand." Nobody hooked on crack got off easily.

Lance was already pretty far gone. He had just graduated high school with zero motivation or plans for college or work. He never mentioned sex, a bad sign for someone his age. He had no friends and was not close to anyone in his family. Drugs seemed to be his only interest. He was getting everything he needed from them: an escape from pain and an almost romantic-sounding intoxication. When he was straight, he was depressed and completely alone, a lone wolf and oddball with a good brain that he was wasting. His days were a revolving door of taking and selling drugs in the low-class, drug-infested sections of Long Island near railroad stations. He told me that when he got stoned he would get lost in primal rages, screaming, "The world sucks."

At our second session, Lance confirmed that he had paid off the drug dealers and was no longer frightened they would kill him. Why the hell couldn't he have figured this out himself? I suspected that, at eighteen, Lance's drug use had already altered his brain chemistry, but I didn't feel he was beyond help. I was a fan of the neurology book *The Brain That Changes Itself*, by psychiatrist Norman Doidge, which argued that the brain can rewire itself, even in the face of catastrophic trauma.

Lance kept showing up week after week, which gave me hope. He shared his interest in philosophy, touting anthropologist Robert Murphy's *The Dialectics of Social Life*, arguing Murphy's point that we are too subjective to understand anything, and, thus, all knowledge is a myth. Lance had a passion for underground novelists John Fowles and William Gass. His favorite book was the little-known *Nog* by Rudolf Wurlitzer. We had sophisticated conversations; I wanted to appeal to his intellectual pride.

To figure out the roots of his addictions, I asked about his past. Lance was the oldest of three kids born close in age to a young, naive mother and emotionally removed father. Neither parent appeared to be addicted or depressed. Lance's offbeat, cerebral outlook had never fit in with his family, school, or neighborhood. Had he been lost from the start? I recalled a scene in a Western movie about a cold, heartless, and evil cowboy. "Why is he so angry?" one rancher asked another. "Because he was born," was the answer.

Like other patients I'd seen, I guessed that Lance had been fed, sheltered, and given a vague familial love, but his parents had not seen, listened, accepted, or understood who he really was. He had never been at peace. Smoking, drinking, and using drugs at age thirteen was his self-medication, the only way he soothed himself. He ranted against the inanity and materialism of the suburbs and all it stood for; he only felt happy while high on crack. I pointed out to Lance that he did not have to feel happy to lead a meaningful existence, a tenet I'd pretty much based *my* entire life on.

"If you can't feel happiness, what else is there, man?" he asked. A typical addict, he saw his only choices as elation or misery.

"You're forgetting there's the possibility of meaning," I told him.

For people who have experienced severe trauma and family addiction, as I have, being happy, as many define it, is simply not an option. Trying to pursue conventional contentment is futile. The only way to generate ongoing happiness is to use a substance to get there. So you have to give up all hope of being blissful, revolve your life around rational rules, and aim for suffering and living well, and meaningfully.

With crack, Lance believed he had access to a beautiful, transcendental experience that provided the illusion of happiness. It was as if he had a portal into God's hands and I was telling him not to use the portal. He felt like I was taking away the only joy he would ever get. This was my conundrum with Lance.

I explained that, counterintuitively, when you give up trying to re-create a fantasy bliss by chasing happiness, it suddenly opens up many new possibilities. You can quit your addiction, stop expecting to feel a typical, unrealistic, continual state of joy, exchange the extreme highs and lows for balance, redefine success, and become much more successful. Instead of pursuing the self-centered feelings that a bad habit satisfies, you can base your existence around what you believe is significant. Ultimately that will give you a deeper satisfaction that will eventually make you feel better in an adult, realistic way.

"Never heard that one before. So I shouldn't aim to be happy?" Lance asked, showing skeptical curiosity, engaged by anything weird or unorthodox. "You're saying the only way to get happiness is to shun it? You bullshitting me or you really believe this?"

"Do you think I would lie to you about an important addiction theory?" I asked.

"Well, you haven't bullshitted me yet," he said and laughed.

I told Lance that, for me, it's important to be a helpful therapist who connects with my patients on a deep level, give to charity, and take good care of my children. I feel satisfaction being able to put their needs before my own. Rather than chase after superficial, conventional feelings of happiness, I have low expectations when it comes to happy emotional states. Instead of expecting to maintain joy, I have learned to greatly appreciate even fleeting moments of pleasure. Especially when I make a conscious decision to wrap my world around what I find meaningful, happiness notwithstanding.

"Ah, but what if there's no such thing as meaning?" Lance asked, smirking. Then he launched into an argument for nihilism.

The sixty-four-million-dollar question with Lance was: What was meaningful to *him*? A remote, antiromantic cynic, he expressed no ambitions in work or love, had no friends or social life, and refused to go to AA or NA meetings. Since he did come out of his shell with me, I hoped our link might help. I conveyed that I cared deeply for him, that what he did mattered to me, that I did not want him to get hurt or killed. Eventually I became important to him, perhaps because I was interested in his cynicism and theories, which he had not shared with anyone else. As a present he brought me a first edition of *Nog*, the 1969 "headventure" described as "somewhere between psychedelic Superman and Samuel Beckett." Knowing that *Nog* meant so much to Lance, the fact that he wanted to share it meant a lot to me. I put it in a prominent place on my bookshelf, where Lance saw it every time he came to my office.

"It presents a different view of reality than anybody else's," he told me.

"That's what you're all about," I said and he agreed.

I suggested Lance keep a journal of when he was using and how he felt before, during, and after he took drugs. Smart and articulate, he enjoyed this, producing Jack Kerouac kind of rambling, rough-and-tumble prose. He wrote about the dark side of Long Island, including how, while scoring crack, he spread his house keys out on his fist, in between his fingers, so that the ends of the keys protruded. That was because he was small and if anybody tried to hurt or rob him he could cut his or her face with the keys' jagged ends.

After six months I asked Lance to try to go without freebasing for as long as he could. He lasted a few days at a time, then a whole week, but the depression he experienced was so profound he became suicidal. "Why bother?" he said. "Everything else in life is complete, unadulterated shit."

When Lance was first getting straight he stopped reading; he lost his powers of concentration. He was less angry but also less alive. He was lethargic and tired all the time. I reassured him that his energy would come back after the withdrawal subsided. In the worst depths of despair, he saw me twice a week.

The next year I was pleased when he was able to stay off crack for five months, a great achievement. During this time, he enrolled in English, philosophy, and writing classes that he enjoyed at a local university. He took a part-time job at a highbrow book store where he voraciously started to read books again.

But while Lance's life was improving, mine was in upheaval. In 1993, after treating him for four years, everything changed for me. This was the year that my wife and I divorced, my mentor threw me out of his inner circle, I left my Long Island home, and moved my practice to the city. Wanting Lance to continue therapy, I asked him to visit my new Greenwich Village office. But he never came.

I later realized it was unrealistic and unfair to expect Lance to adapt to such a new world. For someone getting off of drugs in the suburbs, perhaps Manhattan presented too many obstacles and temptations. Recovering addicts are not at all flexible and rely on repetitive rituals (like therapy sessions or meetings at the exact same time every week). Some cannot go with the flow; the flow leads to using again. Effective addiction treatment is similar to being in a detox center, where every move and meal is micromanaged. Changing the routine of our cocoon of therapy was impossible for Lance. Also, like many addiction patients, he had extreme trouble with closeness. I felt badly that he saw my move as abandonment. If he chose to travel to the city, it would be an explicit admission that he needed me, and a statement about the intimacy that we were establishing, which was unfortunately intolerable for him at this stage.

In the perfect scenario for an addiction patient, a therapist would remain in the same place forever. I recommended another psychologist; Lance wasn't interested. I called him a number of times. We had long, winding talks, yet intermittent phone sessions weren't the same as our in-person appointments. Alas it wasn't possible for him to come to my new office or for me to commute back there. After a while we lost touch. I feared that without regular treatment Lance would relapse.

Unfortunately, relapsing is an integral part of addiction treatment. If an addict tells me he has had a relapse, I do not berate him, express anger, or admit that I feel disappointment (though of course

I do). I reassure him it's normal, knowing that feeling understood and deeply cared for is actually the best way to combat addiction.

In Freud's famous theory of the personality, the id represents a primitive drive that follows the pleasure principle: if it makes me feel good, I do it. The superego acts as the conscience, the naysayer, the rule maker. The ego mediates between two. I find that addicts do not have a strong ego that can referee between their powerful, often childlike desires and the parental voice of admonishment that exists in their heads.

So an alcoholic will drink throughout an entire night, unable to stop. The minute he wakes up, he will kick himself for how stupid and self-indulgent he was the night before. But there is no adult decision-making process that can halt the drive to drink more and to feel less pain while he's on a bender. The same dynamic is at work when one eats a pint of Haagen-Dazs ice cream and feels horrible in the morning. There is no metaphoric moderate mother there to spoon out one scoop, say "that's all," and put the rest away for another day. The choice appears to be all or nothing. There seems to be no such thing as too much comfort for someone who was deprived of nurturing as a child.

At an Alcoholics Anonymous meeting, when a man gets up in front of everyone and says "I have ten years of sobriety," everyone will applaud. The next day if the same man gets up before the group and says "I have eight hours of sobriety," everyone will similarly clap again with the same enthusiasm. The slip is not the focus. Obviously after ten years, the man who has only been sober for eight hours had a relapse the night before. But the group does not embody an angry, scolding parent. The brilliant people who invented twelve-step programs understood that the punishing voice of the superego will make an addict feel guilty and bad about what he or she has done, but will not help him or her regulate or quit the substance he or she relies on. In fact, guilt and low self-loathing drive people to drink more, not less. Instead, a nonjudgmental set of rules and regulations (what AA calls "steps") must be applied to stand in for the moderating influence of the ego and restore sanity.

At one point in the middle of our treatment, Lance had stopped showing up for therapy appointments. I left several phone messages on his machine. Finally, on my next message, I said "Listen, I know what is going on here. You're using drugs, you're in really bad shape, and you feel so stupid and guilty that you cannot bear to call me. Call me anyway. You think I hate you, but I don't. You think I'm sick of you, but I am not. There is nothing you can do to get me to condemn you. I forgive you all your sins. I just want to hear that you are okay." I was relieved when he came back.

———————

While researching this book, I wondered what happened to Lance. I revisted *Nog*, which had been on my bookshelf for many years. I had not spoken to Lance in more than a decade. I feared the worst. Had he died of a drug overdose? Was he in jail? Had he disappeared without a trace? I looked up his mother's number in my files and tried it. She answered the phone and remembered me. She said that Lance was living in a nearby suburb. I told her I was writing about addictions, had thought of Lance and his therapy, and asked if she could update me more.

She said Lance had been completely drug-free for two full years after our therapy. Unfortunately since then he had been using crack, drinking, and smoking cigarettes off and on. He was able to work full-time for his father's business. He had digestive problems but was otherwise shockingly healthy for somebody who freebased. Four years earlier he married a woman the family thought highly of. Lance's wife did not understand the extent of his drug problems, but she was clean herself, and loved him.

"I now identify Lance as my handicapped child," Mrs. T. said.

That seemed a good way to view the situation, similar to how twelve-step programs instruct relatives to deal with loved ones in the throes of addictions. You admit there is a serious problem then detach yourself, invoking rules, principles, and guidelines so that when the addict deteriorates (as they often do), they do not tear the whole family apart.

I appreciated Mrs. T.'s candor. Of course I would have preferred to hear that Lance was entirely drug-free, but I was gratified he was off drugs for two years after our therapy, the longest time he'd been clean since he was a teenager, and that he was married, allowing intimacy into his life. I thought it was good that Lance could stay off of drugs intermittently, which implied he could exert enough restraint over his addiction to function. That was very rare with crack.

The intelligent way that his mother spoke about his addiction was a significant improvement for her. It showed that she was no longer in denial and that Lance had an advocate who understood the depths of his problem. Although obviously still tormented and unable to stay completely clean, Lance may no longer be so alone.

"Tell Lance that I found his book *Nog* and think about him with great affection," I told her. "Please tell him to call me and drop by for a visit. I won't charge him."

After I hung up the phone, I took the book from my shelf, looking for information on the author. All it said was he "lived nowhere in particular." The back described it as "a journey without end, a journey through time past, toward time present, a journey of one man without history, without tradition." I realized it was a story about Lance. No wonder it was his favorite.

IN CASE OF RELAPSE

1. Don't say "I've already ruined everything so it doesn't matter" and go on a worse binge or bender, taking even more drugs, alcohol, cigarettes, or food.

2. Late at night before you go to sleep, get rid of the alcohol, cigarettes, marijuana, or junk food that might entice you to continue the substance abuse in the morning.

3. Call your core pillars and make an appointment. Discuss your digression immediately. Keeping it secret will make it poison-

ous and more problematic. Getting it out in the open will normalize it and allow you to move on faster.

4. In your journal, try to figure out what exactly triggered the relapse.

5. See what you can do to make sure it doesn't happen again. If you were at a party when you used, quit going to parties for a while. If a specific person gave you drugs, avoid that person; if you can't, minimize contact or try to talk on the phone or email instead.

6. The next morning, start over. Begin a cleansing ritual right when you wake up, whether it's saying a serenity prayer, putting on the nicotine patch, going to a recovery meeting, or making an appointment with a doctor or core pillar.

7. Give yourself a healthy present for starting over: a massage, manicure, pedicure, a trip to your favorite bookstore, or lunch with a special friend.

8. Forgive yourself.

CHAPTER 18

THE DANGERS OF ADDICTION THERAPY: ALCOHOL, VIOLENCE

"I can't work with Bob, he's too dangerous. He's a violent alcoholic," Stan, a fellow New York therapist, told my answering machine. Of all the phone messages I listened to at my office that morning, this one definitely caught my attention. It was a Monday, the beginning of January 2002. "He is just not appropriate for my private practice," Stan continued. "I thought maybe somebody at The Village Institute could try to help him."

I already knew from Stan's message that I was not going to pass along this patient, Bob, to one of the therapists I had trained. Bob was mine. A dangerous and out-of-control addict was just my type. It was home territory, where I grew up. It was what I knew best, as if staring him in the eye was a way to confront—and tame—the dark side of myself.

All my life I've gravitated toward emotional darkness. I loved the Chaos Theory, as well as extreme sports. I always found myself trying to forge an alliance with chaos. With a mother who was a raging alcoholic, I guessed that chaos and my penchant for white-water kayaking down dangerous rivers were metaphors for my turbulent relationship with her. During all the years she refused to return my calls and letters, I hoped to eventually convince her to meet with me.

If I was even handed and patient, I thought that was a possibility. If I kept fighting against her, I feared I would live and die miserably, re-creating the terror she'd made me feel as a child.

I thought of Melanie Klein's assessment about how haunted an adult could be if he did not feel adequate maternal love early in life. Of course I had to always make sure that I was not merely projecting my own personal issues onto my patients. Noting how terribly addicts whom I'd treated had suffered from a rupture in the bond between child and mother helped me understand why they were so afraid of dependency. I could use my past pain as the basis for empathy.

Two days after the phone message about the dangerous addict, Bob himself left the message: "I don't need therapy. I'm just calling because my buddy Pete told me to." His tone seemed aggressive, tough, and arrogant. Although he went on to say he was married and worked as a successful freelance TV news producer in Manhattan, he sounded as if he had borrowed the language and swagger of a Robert De Niro gangster. I called Bob back and we made an afternoon appointment for the next Monday.

When Bob walked in my office, I stared at him. He was tough and good looking, thirty-three years old, dark, intense, strong, muscular, and unshaven. He stood about five foot eight, a shorter, stockier George Clooney. He looked like he could get any woman he wanted and he knew it. When he sat down on my couch, I thought, "He could kill me." This guy in my office was street. Bob could take me and he flaunted it. He had experienced naked fury up close; he carried it around with him. In a physical contest, I would be no match.

I did not usually judge myself by my size, weight, or muscles (or lack thereof). I was a basically cerebral six-foot, 165-pound, fifty-year-old WASP with degrees in philosophy and psychology. I did not normally feel competitive with my male patients. Most of them could beat me up one-two-three if they had a mind to. As an Upper East Side private-school kid growing up on Park Avenue, I had been lonely, scrawny, and nonathletic. I'd hidden inside, where my only hobbies were painting and listening to 78 RPM opera records I had taken from my mother's collection. Growing up I'd play Puccini's *Madame Butterfly* over and over, which I had found calming through the domestic storms of my childhood.

In nature, I would be the antler type: escape to survive, do not stand your ground, and risk getting hurt. Consumed by emotional conflicts, I avoided physical fights. I could not remember ever throwing a punch or getting into a brawl. In high school, I became good at long-distance running, a safe, solitary sport. During my undergraduate years at Amherst College, I tried my hand at the relatively genteel games of squash and tennis and I was a decent softball pitcher. Although I later took up skiing and rafting, I never went near the more macho contact sports of football, hockey, boxing, or wrestling.

When I was twenty-four and attempting to prove my mettle, I embarked on a thousand-mile walking journey through France and Spain on a medieval pilgrimage road. I came to a perilous stretch where three wild dogs surrounded me. My friend, Conrad, who had walked this same path, had warned me about this stretch of road and about the dogs that roamed there. He had told me to keep a knife in my hand. "If the dogs smell your fear, they will attack. But if they know you will cut their throats, they will leave you alone," Conrad had said. Sure enough on the trail, the wild dogs were circling, ready to pounce. I had my knife ready. At that moment I had never been so prepared for violence. I knew with absolute certainty that if they came closer, I would cut their throats without a moment's hesitation. I found myself actually hoping that the snarling beasts would come closer; I was ready. They backed off.

That was when I realized that I was not a pure intellectual. I was a slightly built, cerebral, urban pacifist, but I could kill if I had to. I had strong survival instincts. I tried to summon up those same instincts with Bob.

"So if you don't need therapy, what are you doing here?" I asked, bluntly.

"I'm having anger issues."

"What's making you angry?" I asked.

"I'm troubled by something that happened between me and my younger sister, Sally," Bob admitted.

"You don't seem like a stranger to trouble to me," I said.

I was trying to be confrontational to show him the side of me that wasn't your average, passive therapist who would let him control the mood and tenor of therapy. I wanted to let Bob know that I understood who he was and that I could be a worthy adversary. A classy doctor's office on Lower 5th Avenue with red carpet and plush pillows seemed an odd place for a pissing contest, yet like those wild dogs in Spain, if Bob saw I meant business, I hoped he would back down. Maybe he would even follow me down the path he needed to go.

He laughed in an all-knowing, sarcastic sneer that seemed to say "You don't know the half of it, buddy."

"Let me put it this way," he told me. "If I'm at a bar and a guy looks at my wife funny, I'll tell him 'You want to fuck with her, you're gonna have to fuck with me.' The guy might be bigger. He might be stronger. But I have internal power. My emotion is like a nuclear power plant. When I turn it on, the biggest and the strongest get crushed by me. By my bare hands. And after my fists pulverize him, I can always take out my gun and blow him away."

He was clearly not boasting; he was speaking facts. He was not an educated, verbally sophisticated guy. He operated on instinct and tone. He hadn't yet told me what his addiction was. The mention of being in a bar suggested alcoholism. But the more pressing problem was his inclination toward violence.

"Do you have a gun?" I asked, concerned. "Where is it?"

"Why do you want to know?" He was still smirking, challenging me.

"If you've got a gun, that scares me. I won't talk to someone I'm afraid of," I said. "I would be watching my words and monitoring everything I say. You need somebody who will speak his mind and tell you the brutal truth you don't want to hear."

Bob was scared, scary, and made a habit of repelling anybody who came near him. He was chasing away exactly what he so desperately needed—intimacy from people who could be there for him. I have found that many addicts displayed this kind of emotional distance, a stubbornness rooted in fear and a strong, off-putting, or annoying public persona that would not let anyone get too close. If you ever encountered an extreme case like this, I would advise seeking the help of a doctor, addiction expert, or an AA leader trained in breaking down the person's barriers in a healthy, safe environment.

Even as an expert in the field with thirty years of experience, I admit I was afraid of Bob, yet I spoke calmly and objectively. I didn't back down from telling him the truth.

"If you want my help, your first job here is to make me not afraid," I said. "If you can't do that, my hands are tied." I already knew I could be helpful to him. So did he. He caught my tone.

"My gun is at home," he said.

I guessed it was unregistered. "The next time we meet, I want you to bring me your gun, without bullets in it. Bring the bullets in a separate container," I said.

"What are you going to do with it?" he asked.

"I have a close friend named Donny who is a detective in the NYPD. I'll give it to him," I said. "He won't ask where I got it. He'll just get rid of it. Gone. No questions. No names."

After years entrenched in intense addiction therapy, my professional demeanor had become much more aggressive and nontraditional. In 1983, when Courtney, my first Manhattan patient, came to see me with an out-of-control cocaine problem, it did not even occur to me to ask her to postpone the ill-timed trip overseas she was planning to take. I was more likely to adhere to the typical boundaries and limitations of my profession. But now, almost twenty years later, I did not hesitate to order Bob, an angry, alcoholic patient I had just met, to bring me his weapon. I knew it seemed like I was acting in a John Wayne movie, yet I had learned that to be effective I had to be much more assertive with difficult patients, knowing that was what was often needed to wrestle away addictions. It was not an easy process. I would rather risk stretching the law, with my friend Donny's collaboration, than have this man get drunk and blow his brains out. Or blow someone else's brains out—like mine.

Horrible anxiety states caused by missing mothers. Chaotic mood swings. A world filled with darkness and danger. Was it any wonder why I was so drawn to the addict population? These were my people.

"Okay," Bob nodded. The rational side of him did not really want to use his gun on somebody he cared about, or himself. He looked a bit relieved, as if he could finally get rid of the evidence from a crime scene. I wondered how many times the gun had been used before. Had he already shot somebody?

I've argued with colleagues that successful addiction treatment often has to be brazen, out of the box and unconventional. Patients have to take action and make changes much more quickly than your garden-variety analysis or else they will get high or stoned and drive a car with kids in the backseat. Or worse.

Along with external changes, it was also essential to get to the inner roots of a substance problem. To stop it, you had to figure out what hurt so much that made someone need to self-medicate many times daily, often for decades. As a psychoanalyst, I was always curious about a patient's family and asked Bob a quick succession of questions. For a guy who came off like a hoodlum, there was surprisingly little abuse, addiction, or violence in his background. There was just massive neglect, not an uncommon breeding ground in which addictions frequently develop.

Bob was the only son in a lower-middle-class, Staten Island, Irish-Catholic clan with three sisters. His mother was a housewife who sounded sweet, nice, and full of denial. His father, a blue-collar worker, was a hands-off dad who was passive and set no limits. I had grown up one of four children, too. Yet unlike my parents, who had divorced when I was eleven years old, Bob's parents were still together. Even so, Bob had grown up in a house with no rules, lawless, as my home was. As someone who had experienced the intense absence of parental love and protection, I once again guessed that what Bob really yearned for was a father figure.

He said he "pulled in about 90 grand a year" on different projects, despite his drinking problem. I am often amazed at how much people can drink while being highly functional. Alcoholics can build up an astounding tolerance for holding their liquor without getting drunk.

"So what happened with your sister, Sally?" I asked him.

Bob chronicled how three months before, his twenty-three-year-old youngest sister, Sally, had committed suicide. She had hanged herself with a leather belt in their parents' house. It was right after the World Trade Center attacks, which had greatly affected Sally. She had been diagnosed years before with bipolar disorder. The whole story, which took several sessions to fully uncover, was that Sally had come to Bob's house the night before she had killed herself. Emotionally unbalanced for years, she was once again threatening suicide. This time Bob lost all patience and pulled out his gun.

"Okay, I'm going to kill you right now," he said. He dragged her to the bathroom and made her look at herself in the mirror. In a desperate effort to knock sense into her, Bob had put her in a choke hold and put the gun to her head. "You can stop threatening suicide," he screamed at her. "Say your last words now cause I'm going to blow your brains out!"

"Go ahead, do it. Please," she said.

Not the response he wanted.

When she really did take her own life the next day, Bob blamed himself. Then he put the blame on Sally's therapist. Then he drank himself into a stupor with whiskey. Though neither of his parents drank or did drugs, Bob admitted that he had started drinking when he was twelve years old.

I often note that emotionally addicts remain at the age they were when they started using. They turned to substances to deal with intense discomfort and conflicts they had never even started to resolve.

They try to erase their emotional turmoil by drinking, smoking, gambling, or eating their pain away. That never gets rid of any of their problems. In fact, it makes everything worse.

Bob sister's violent demise was the event that motivated him to call me. In AA parlance, he'd hit bottom. The fun drinking façade was gone, and the consequences of his habit had become intolerable. That is when addicts often ask for help—when the horrors of using become worse than the horrors of not using.

I told Bob my mantra that underlying every substance problem I had ever seen was a deep depression that felt unbearable. I reassured him that it was not actually unbearable; it just felt that way. Addicts who had used substances since they were teenagers had never developed normal coping skills. Using became their only way to cope. The point of addiction therapy or AA was to give them the language and skills to unravel the rage and confusion brewing beneath their bad habits.

"How much do you drink?" I asked him. Although I tried never to place a value judgment on addictive behavior or make therapy seem like an inquisition, the nitty-gritty of drug or alcohol use was essential for a patient to verbalize. It countered the denial and made it more real. Plus confessing really was good for an addict's soul and sanity. It made him or her feel less alone.

"A bottle of Jack Daniels every other night," he answered.

"I bet it's more than that," I said.

I wanted Bob to know what I was thinking. There had to be no lies, no games, and no deception. He had to tell me everything, be an open book; there was strength in honesty. I would do the same. I repeated my rule: that in order to get and stay happy and healthy, he should lead the least secretive life that one can.

On the other side of the couch, I did not believe in being a blank slate like many therapists did. I felt it was okay to present myself as a complicated person with whom the addict had to contend. The way most effective addiction treatment went, eventually he would have to transfer his alcohol dependency onto a human being he could depend on. I aimed to fill that role. As a child with an abusive alcoholic mother, nobody had come to my rescue. As an adult, I wanted to be the person I wished would have saved me from the troubles of my childhood.

Although sometimes an addict can quit taking a substance in one session, it is never a short or simple process to get and stay clean. Cigarettes, alcohol, or drugs often do a brilliant job of making everything difficult seem better and easier to deal with in the short-term. They act as antidepressants, appetite suppressors, mood stabilizers, and emotional protectors. You can always have a pack of cigarettes in your pocket or a bottle of pills in your medicine chest or fancy booze in your liquor cabinet. Because human beings are much less dependable and controllable, substances are more consistent than friends, family, and lovers. They were *always* available for you. If you run out, you can easily go buy some more.

If you give credence to my philosophy, then nothing is ever going to feel as good as a child getting his or her mother's protection and adoration. For those not lucky enough to experience that kind of loving care in their first few years of childhood, nothing compensates for it later in life. At a certain point, that window to internalize unconditional love closes. Even if you do not believe that an early lack of love has anything to do with substance abuse, a large part of all addicts' recovery involves feeling intense sadness. They have to go through a mourning process, partly for the time they wasted drinking or getting high. It is not unlike grieving for someone close who has died. They have to confront a huge empty space inside.

Bob had been filling that empty space with whiskey.

"Should I do what I normally do and double the amount of alcohol you're admitting to get to the truth?" I asked him.

"Let me put it this way." He smirked again. "Double it every other day and figure I'm telling you the truth half of the time."

He was smart and spoke in a sly, backhanded way, as if he was so used to lying that he could only sneak in the truth.

"I'm not impressed," I told him. I did not want him to think he had startled or shocked me. In decades doing addiction therapy, I had heard worse, though if the average person polished off a whole bottle of Jack Daniels in one sitting, he could wind up in the hospital, or dead. "You are drinking an enormous amount. And I know the reason you drink so much." I said this very slowly. "It's because you can't do it unless you drink.'" I did not specify whether "it" was sex, surviving, working, or being a tough guy. It was all of them.

He agreed to bring the gun in and see me once a week. Before he left, he stood up and said, "You're not like the rest of them," like De Niro. I was not sure if I was ever going to see this guy again.

But the next session he did show up, albeit gunless, offering an excuse for why he could not bring his gun in. I agreed to see him for that session but presented him with an ultimatum. If he did not bring in his gun the next time, it was over. I told him I just could not treat a loose cannon who drank as much as he did while harboring a weapon he could hold over my head. He was sure to kill someone and maybe it would be me.

On the third session, Bob brought the gun in a metal box. The bullets were in a separate container. It was wrapped in rags. He handed it to me sheepishly. While I sensed that giving me the gun was an important step, it seemed like an intimate expression of dependency that felt humiliating to him. So I did not focus on it or ask how he felt. Instead I said, "This was the right thing to do," putting it in gunslinger terms (black and white, good guys and bad guys) and past tense, as if the worst part was over and there was only one place to go from here.

I carefully placed the gun and bullets in my cabinet, where I had previously stashed a knife, heroin, sleeping pills, and antianxiety medication I had confiscated from other patients. When I kept drugs and weapons in my office, I always told at least one colleague, along with my detective friend, Donny. He promised he would vouch for me in case the contraband was found and I needed an alibi. Luckily I never did.

"Now you and I can get to work," I told Bob, implying we were a team.

The rest of the session he spoke about his sister, Sally. He was the closest person in her life and felt responsible for her death. After Bob left, I called Donny, who sent over a plain-clothes colleague. I gave him the gun, which I never saw again.

Bob's sister's last night continued to haunt him. How could it not? He had threatened to kill her. All his attempts to help her had just made the situation worse, which unfortunately was not unusual when addictions were involved.

"The whole scene was crazy," I told him. "Sally was out of control with intense, confused, chaotic feelings. I know you were trying a radical, extreme technique, but if someone is determined to kill him- or herself, nothing you can do will help."

He kept repeating that he had partly caused his sister's death. While I did not agree with him, I did not exonerate him either. If his guilt would motivate him to get sober then it served a good purpose. At our next therapy appointment, Bob broke down and cried. He was a person who had immediate access to a reservoir of violence and rage that had become part of who he was. Addicts often have many compulsions working at the same time. If Bob was addicted to something other than alcohol, it was sex. For Bob, screwing around was reckless, random, and in the moment. He wanted sex, he got it, then he threw the girl away.

I asked how he could treat his wife this way. I learned that Anne was a thirty-two-year-old, soft-spoken nurse. Ironically Bob feared that *she* was having an affair. If Anne was seeing someone, he was partly responsible because he had been treating her so horribly. Self-victimization was rarely helpful in cases where people were causing or perpetuating their own misery and I had little or no patience for it. I told Bob that Anne was so neglected there was no right or wrong anymore. If she was seeing another man, he had to blame himself for forcing her to seek closeness elsewhere. If she was not seeing anyone else, he still had to take responsibility for ignoring her terribly.

"It's okay for a man to have affairs, but not a woman," he said, sharing his sexist view and looking like a hurt little boy.

"Not the way you've been treating her. You're a criminal in all of these proceedings," I said. "You have been forcing her hand."

When he told me he had raised his fist and almost hit her one night, I feared he might wind up being physically abusive and insisted he move out and get his own place for a while.

"Why shouldn't *she* move out?" he asked. "It's my apartment. I pay for it."

"It's time that you step up to the plate and start being a good, generous man who does the right thing," I said.

Concerned that Anne would misinterpret his moving out and think he was leaving her, I suggested she accompany him to a therapy session. I often asked patients to bring in the spouse, parents, or children with whom they were having trouble. That way I could get a better sense of what they were dealing with, who would hinder their recovery, and who might be a core pillar available to help.

Anne came with him to the next session. She was pretty and petite, wearing a blouse and skirt and looking very feminine. They seemed like they had been through the war; they were battle weary. I explained to her that it was my idea that Bob move out. Though he had never hit her, I wanted to make sure it stayed that way. He had to learn how to be respectful, the only way their marriage would last.

Although he was drinking, abusive, violent, and neglectful, she still loved her husband and did not want to lose him or their marriage. After that session, I felt no need to see her again. She was passive and clearly was not going to be blazing the trail here. Bob would either do the right thing or not. He moved out a few months later.

I pushed him to keep a journal of every substance he took, including alcohol, cocaine, pot, even aspirin for a headache, and allergy medication, an essential step in recovery. I insisted he write down everything he put into his mouth that could alter his mood, even caffeine and sugar. On one page, I explained, I wanted a diary.

On the opposite page I wanted him to write exactly what he was feeling right before he took a drink or a pill.

This technique makes addicts conscious of what they ingest and why. It can break through their denial and teaches them how to connect their usage of substances to their emotions. It introduces them to the existence of their new internal lives. I assure them I will read it but not judge them. It's important for addicts to acknowledge and admit the specific facts, getting rid of denial and defensiveness.

When Bob asked, I spoke of being on the other side, as a one-time pack-a-day smoker who knew how wonderful it felt to use and how hard it was to give up. Also, as the son of an alcoholic, I shared stories about the havoc and agony of addiction I'd witnessed as a child. "One person's substance abuse can destroy an entire family forever," I told him, speaking from my own experience. "In fact, I can trace my broken marriage, my parents' estrangement, and all my siblings' divorces back to my mother's inability to stop drinking."

Many well-respected analysts prefer to remain neutral and blank, but again here was another case where it seemed more helpful to be open and transparent. I believe that a therapist's anonymity does not really matter. Remember, Freud himself frequently socialized with his clients outside of treatment, having them to tea at his home, speaking to them freely about his own life.

Since I was a broken record, constantly reiterating that recovering addicts had to depend on people and not substances, I wanted my patients to know the complications involved in that prospect. So when I had to cancel a session with Bob and he asked why, I told the truth: my young daughter had gotten sick at camp, my wife was away for the day, and I had to go pick up my child immediately. I thought it was helpful for patients to see and understand that all human beings were complicated, unpredictable, and uncontrollable. It was okay to feel—and express—disappointment or anger or hurt towards me.

Within his first month of treatment, Bob began to see that he drank in order to cope with his inner turmoil. "I came home from work stressed out, tired, and in a rage and I picked up the Jack

Daniels and I knew I was going to feel okay very soon," he told me. Then he sarcastically added, "So, doc, you're right. I drink to cope."

"So you're too weak to face your emotions when you're straight?" I asked.

I said that to challenge him, to get his fighting spirit, his aggression, and his immense pride on our side. I tried to speak his tough guy language and I could tell it engaged him. He liked it. He would say "I know what you're doing; you're trying to hook me."

"I am telling you the truth and it's the truth that's hooking you."

I did not want to embarrass him, but I also did not want him to win the battle over me; then he would lose his best ally. I had started feeling close to him, as a friend with fatherly feelings. Maybe even motherly feelings were getting thrown in. There was something in Bob that I recognized. He was a smart guy with a big heart and endless amounts of pain inside like I used to have. In my mind, he was not unlike me. I was sure I could help him through this identification (which is why finding a core pillar who has been through recovery is so useful). Since I saw him as me at an earlier stage, I would always know more than he did. I had spent twenty-five years trying to understand and work with my own chaotic self. So I had twenty-five years on him.

After six weeks of seeing me, Bob realized how he was using booze to numb his difficult feelings. Then I asked him to go one whole day without drinking. I use this exercise when a patient is full of denial and says, "My use isn't a problem, I don't have to stop" or "I can stop anytime I want."

"So stop using for a week," I challenged. Usually an alcoholic can't even stop for a day. Bob stopped for twenty-four hours, an encouraging sign.

"It was horrible," he said. "I don't think I can do this."

I next suggested he go to an Alcoholics Anonymous meeting. I told him he did not have to like it, he did not have to believe in it and he could feel uncomfortable with all the "God" stuff. I often recommend AA highly since statistically addicts who go to recovery meetings get clean in much greater numbers. The vast majority of people who agreed to see me once a week and supplemented it with at least two weekly meetings became sober. I did not fight the numbers. But Bob refused. He had problems admitting weakness in public and asking for help. He had problems with crowds. He was a loner. I felt that at some point he would need to find support in a community. Still, he did much better one-on-one than in group settings. I wondered if it had to do with sibling rivalry. As one of four children who never felt loved, who was I to argue or deny him individual attention? My rule was that he could do anything as long as it worked, and this seemed to be working.

After four months of seeing me weekly, Bob stopped drinking completely. But he felt no illusions of happiness or "a pink cloud," the temporary sensation of euphoria and well-being characteristic of those who are new to sobriety that rarely lasts. Bob hated life without alcohol, as some people initially do. He was in deep intense pain, which, in my book, is a perfectly normal and healthy response to quitting. He was letting himself suffer, allowing the feelings to surface instead of obliterating them with mind-numbing substances. He saw me more often, sometimes twice a week. He started to exercise at the gym. He moved out to Long Island and ran on the beach to get rid of stress and anxiety.

There was a big, boozy bar scene in the Hamptons over the summer. I suggested that he avoid bars and parties filled with inebriated people at all costs, but Bob insisted he could handle it. He pulled it off. He socialized with his friends but drank only soda and water. He was the designated driver. What he saw in his old crowd shocked him—the dishonesty and recklessness he had never noticed before. He witnessed how the drunk and drugged-out people he used to hang out with were abusing and hurting each other. He was still seducing young women but without the same intensity as in the past. Without alcohol, his old routine was losing its luster.

Bob decided to take three months off work. I encouraged him because this removed him from his stressful environment. Sometimes patients needed to do that. It was like going to a rehab center but better because his sobriety was not dependent on doctors, nurses, and other patients in group therapy. Then he would not be shocked when he got out into the real world.

That fall Bob reconciled with his wife. Anne did still not fully trust him, but she let him move back into their apartment. I thought it was a bad decision on her part. "I wish she said no so we would know she was protecting herself and managing you better," I told him.

Addicts benefit from having tough, skeptical people in their lives who do not trust their judgment, who are cynical about their promises, and who have the courage to say no and make the addicts prove themselves. (Again, another reason why an addiction specialist, tough shrink, or AA colleague helps.) Still, Bob was not drinking or doing drugs, so their relationship was much improved. He was writing in his journal every day, taking her out, and telling her more about his feelings.

Six months later, on his birthday, he drank wine during dinner. He thought he could handle having just one glass and tested himself. He was shocked that he immediately wanted to go out and buy a bottle of Jack Daniels. But he didn't. He had a lot of resolve. When he told me about it, I didn't overreact or show disappointment. He has not had a drink since. In retrospect, his relapse was not a bad thing because he learned from it. He found out how powerful any liquor was.

I do not believe in the school of thought that allows former alcoholics to drink once in a while. I have never seen it work. In my experience addictions never remain status quo. If untreated, they always get worse. The user ends up needing more and the same amount affects them less. The endless need is never satisfied. It is only a matter of time before the drinking spirals out of control.

Bob stopped sleeping with other women, though he screwed up once. It was the same experience with his alcohol relapse. He'd picked up a model and had a one-night stand that, to his surprise, did not feel good. He realized he could do this for the rest of his life, but it no longer hit the spot. Although I usually pressed for complete honesty, in this case confessing to Anne would not be productive.

She was wounded enough. He had learned from his mistake. He came in that day hating his new life.

"I drink and it doesn't feel good. I have sex with a hot stranger and it doesn't feel good. What am I becoming? A moral human being? A good citizen? I hate good citizens," he lamented. "How can I feel good anymore?"

In January 2004, after two years of treatment, Bob asked me "Can I have a baby?" It was as if he needed a good father who was stronger than he was to tame the lion and give him permission to be an honest, self-respecting husband and dad himself.

"Yes, I think you are able to do that now. Do you see any reason why not?" I asked.

"Because if I have a girl she could get gang raped in Central Park," he said. Although he was sober, he still saw the world as filled with evil and was afraid he wouldn't be able to protect his child.

I talked about the fears I had raising my daughter, son, and stepson. "Your reasons are based on the premise that you are going to be a bad father," I told him. "You won't let your daughter grow up to be reckless and have bad judgment. You'll instill good values in her. You can be a good dad." I reinforced the idea that to do this he would have to stay clean and have strong values himself, setting the example.

At one point, he went to the Adirondacks with his laptop and poured out a full confession about what happened that horrible last night with his sister. It was twenty-five pages, a breakthrough. It was in his own voice, a stream of consciousness where nothing was left out. He could handle all the emotions now. He accepted a certain degree of responsibility, blame, and shame as part of that whole nightmare. He let himself cry when talking about Sally. He soon became closer to his wife.

Finally he told me, "Nothing bad will happen if I have a daughter because I'll be a good father." His wife became pregnant. This made him happy and proud. He gave me a huge cigar and he said, "You know you made this possible."

I took the cigar but did not smoke it. As a former smoker, I know better than to test my luck. I tucked it away in my office cabinet where, two years earlier, I had stashed Bob's weapon. I guessed they were (perhaps phallic?) declarations of our relationship, symbols of the battles we had fought together. When he gave me his gun, it was like saying, "I will trust you with my power." The cigar was a gift of love. I admired his accomplishments, how he had cleaned up his life and held himself with honor and dignity. I felt very close to him, like a father would. (Yes, I know, it's a repetitive theme in my work and life. It reminds me of a John Ashbery poem about how he "becomes what's missing.")

"I'm proud of you," I told Bob.

In the last decade, I continued to see him off and on. He has stayed sober, fixed his marriage, become the protective father of two daughters, and enhanced his career so he is now making $500,000 a year. If my colleague, Stan, saw Bob now, he would not recognize him. Bob had gone from being a violent, dangerous drunk to a mature, rational family man. He was launched.

"It's a fucking miracle," Bob recently told me.

But it was not a miracle. When an addict is ready to turn his life around and seek help, amazing transformations can take place.

CHAPTER 19

STAYING CLEAN AND CAREFUL FOREVER: RECOVERY

Quitting a substance that once soothed you is not a simple process with a beginning, middle, and end. To be successful, an addict must make a lifelong commitment to remain clean and sober. Sometimes, for a very short period, some people immediately feel elated, excited, and relieved to stop smoking, drinking, overeating, or using drugs and experience the previously mentioned phenomenon known as "a pink cloud." But the instinct to use will inevitably pop up, sometimes when least expected.

Although your desire to return to your habit might remain dormant for years, you must understand that it is always there. When it resurfaces, it will be in a moment of weakness, illness, loss, hunger, fatigue, or fear. The death of a loved one, an accident that requires an operation, or the loss of a job or home are all among the major stressful events that can trigger self-destructive actions. No matter how smart or clean you try to stay, calamities will occur that challenge your most healthy instincts. For example, right after the horrible events of 9/11, many former smokers, drinkers, drug users, and overeaters reached for booze, cigarettes, joints, and comfort food, along with what the media labeled "trauma sex," in order to relieve feelings of pain and horror. The world is chaotic and, unfortunately, as recent earthquakes, hurricanes, and tsunamis showed, we cannot control external forces. We can only control ourselves.

When you first start the process of quitting a substance, the AA motto "one day at a time" is helpful because the thought of having to quit forever is too overwhelming. However, once an addict has stayed clean through the day, week, month, year, and decade, even then he or she is not out of the woods. Neurobiological studies regarding addictive pathways have proven their remarkable durability and resilience. So do not fool yourself into thinking that remaining clean will be easy or just hurt for a little while or that you will one day be able to use your substance moderately. In almost all addiction cases, these scenarios are inaccurate and amount to wishful thinking. Wishes lead directly to substances. While your cravings might feel less intense, the loss is not going to disappear. Extreme words like "never" and "forever" do apply. Some rules are *not* meant to be broken. A recovering alcoholic should not go into a bar. A one-time gambler does not belong at a casino in Las Vegas or an OTB parlor for any reason. A formerly obese person should not hang out at a bakery or candy factory. It's black and white. Don't let your mind play tricks on you or your emotions will take over your common sense. The answer is simply no.

Often people who have been off drugs, cigarettes, or alcohol for a while decide to test themselves, thinking they can handle temptation. These tests tend to fail. One former smoker who had spent ten years smoke-free thought he could handle one puff of a cigarette. By the end of the week, he was back smoking a pack a day. An alcoholic patient of mine told me, "I don't know what happened. I just found myself in a bar. I was going to get a soda, but then somebody handed me a beer. I saw my hand pick up the drink and bring it to my mouth . . ." By the end of the night she had consumed nine beers and didn't remember what had transpired between herself and the man who brought her home. In order to not let emotions ambush all the hard work you've done, here are ways to stay vigilant forever.

HOW TO STAY VIGILANT

Keep in touch with your sponsor, addiction specialist, therapist, or doctor for as long as possible, even it is just for once-a-month or once-a-year "tune ups." The specialist can often detect things you can't see. I recall that one patient, who had quit drugs, mentioned presents she had bought for her husband, mother, and mother-in-law. Until I pointed it out, she did not even realize that she had become a shopaholic, using shopping to take her out of herself and her boredom, in the same way she had once used drugs. If you cannot afford to keep regular appointments, ask your therapist if he or she would consider short monthly phone or email check-ins.

If you are feeling like you might go back to your substance, consider going to Alcoholics Anonymous, Gamblers Anonymous, or Weight Watchers meetings. It is easy to find one almost every day in every town, and it will help remind you that you are not alone and help is available. It is easier to stay vigilant with the help of others with similar problems.

Keep in contact with your core pillars and have numbers on hand to call if you are feeling weak. Whether it's a caring relative, a friend who is a former user, your addiction therapist, or a doctor, this will give you an escape plan. Instead of using, ask to meet with him or her for a cup of coffee to talk out what's going on *before* you act on your impulses.

Everything counts, so watch your other habits. Eat as healthily as possible and exercise regularly. Once you have given yourself permission to eat a box of cookies, you are more likely to reach for a cigarette or pill or martini. Even if alcohol was never your problem, one drink lowers your resistance to other substances like cigarettes, drugs, food, and gambling. Recovered alcoholics who smoke have a higher relapse rate.

Get plenty of sleep. If you develop insomnia, do not ignore it. It is serious. Make an appointment to see your addiction specialist or a doctor to remedy the situation. Often the solution is careful use of sleeping aids for a short period of time. Loss of sleep causes loss of control.

Monitor your stress levels. Take into account your vulnerability when making family decisions. For example a recovering addict might not be able to handle being a caretaker to an aging parent or sick child. Taking on a second job or mortgage might sound like a good idea, but think twice before adding anything stressful to your day-to-day routine. Even vacations to unknown locales can cause discomfort and anxiety you don't expect. Always remember the way that you once handled angst—by using—and try not to put yourself in stressful situations you might not be ready to handle.

Wherever you go, have an escape route or a plan to excuse yourself if somebody is using. A former drug addict should not stay at a party where somebody lights up a joint or starts sniffing cocaine. A gambler should not remain at a friend's house if somebody there begins a poker game. If you have had problems drinking and somebody spikes the punch at an event that was supposed to be alcohol-free, get out of there. You can always say, "I'm not feeling well" and take off. If you don't have a car, carry a cell phone with you to summon a spouse, friend, or core pillar to get you to a safety zone quickly.

Take care of yourself before other people. No matter what your spouse, parents, children, and employers need from you, your priority in life from now on must be to stay clean and sober. If you don't, you will be no good to anyone. There is nothing important enough to put your sobriety at risk.

CHAPTER 20

KEEP HOLIDAY "CHEER" FROM TURNING HARMFUL

I was once at a holiday dinner party where a guest whom I knew got drunk and passed out at the table, right in his food. Everyone was silent, stunned, and extremely uncomfortable, not knowing what to do. I calmly said, "Patrick is drunk and his head has fallen into his plate." Everyone felt relieved for the acknowledgement that this bizarre event had happened and also that I did not overreact or judge him or place blame on anyone. This is a good strategy for dealing with an addict in your life. But socializing can get complicated during seasonal festivities, especially when other people's bad habits affect you and your family.

According to the World Health Organization, alcohol abuse kills 2.5 million people each year and 4 percent of all deaths worldwide are attributable to alcohol, greater than the rate caused by HIV/AIDS or tuberculosis. And liquor is not just causing fatalities from cancer, cirrhosis, heart disease, and strokes. New York City Health Department statistics recently showed that nearly 74,000 people came to New York hospitals alone for alcohol-related reasons last year, a 250 percent leap from the year before. That was because binge drinking led to alcohol poisoning, bar fights, drunken spills, and other serious injuries.

The scariest statistics came from a recent international study by a British physician group, which showed alcohol was the most harmful addiction, worse than heroin and crack cocaine, *because of the harm it does others*. So even if you're moderate yourself or sipping virgin Mary's, inebriated revelers in your home and social world are more likely to drive drunk and engage in domestic abuse, and public violence could destroy your dinner, celebration, and your life.

Crack and cocaine are horrible addictions, but the wide availability of liquor to all ages, lack of regulation and awareness, and denial about the severity of the issue worsens the problem. Be aware that society often pushes people to imbibe, advocates drinking, and looks down on people who do not drink. Although you don't want to be an enabler at seasonal dinners and parties, you don't have to play prissy preacher either. Just remember that many people—perhaps some in your own family—have trouble tolerating alcohol and overuse can hurt and kill innocent bystanders. While nobody enjoys being the fun police, it's even less fun to wind up in the emergency room at 3:00 AM. Here are ways to help those with often hidden addiction problems get through the holidays better and thus keep yourself, your family, and everyone around you safer.

HELP OTHERS GET THROUGH THE HOLIDAYS

1. **BE A BAD BARTENDER:** You don't have to feel obligated to share an open bar stocked with every kind of booze to be a great host. Instead, it's fine to just serve wine and beer, or one drink like wine spritzers or eggnog. Have nonalcoholic or lite beer and bottled water handy and an array of special coffees, teas, smoothies, or exotic fruit juices like passion fruit, guava, and pomegranate. This might welcome—and not ostracize—someone struggling to stay off the sauce.

2. **BOOZE ISN'T ALWAYS THE BEST PRESENT:** Yes, Miss Manners says don't show up to someone's home empty handed and guests

love leaving with goody bags and leftovers. But Miss Manners probably didn't tell you, or know, which relatives were in AA or if your host or her daughter might be on the verge of a relapse. So reconsider one-stop shopping at the liquor store for hostess gifts and rethink doggy bags filled with brandy beans and candy rum balls. Instead try mixed nuts, vegetables from your garden, potpourri, or a big bouquet of cherry blossoms—presents never known to be bad influences on anyone (except asthma sufferers).

3. **SAY IT STRAIGHT:** It's never a good idea to directly confront a person who is high or drunk, and interventions require experts to help. On the other hand, if someone close to you has over-imbibed and fallen asleep at the table or put his or her head in their pie—you don't have to be afraid to speak about it to the other guests who have witnessed this awkward situation. Quietly acknowledge it to the other people nearby with a calm, accurate statement, something along the lines of saying, "Unfortunately Aunt Jenny drank too much again." If you've been in AA, Al-Anon, Al-Ateen, or therapy yourself to deal with your own addiction issues or alcoholic relatives, talk about it so others with alcoholic relatives might feel less alone and safer opening up.

4. **CHANGE IT UP:** For years your family has sat around guzzling beer and watching football or gorging on nachos and margaritas. That can lead to boisterous spats, bellyaches, and blackouts. It's time to create a different ritual. Why not suggest a long walk among the leaves? Or a bicycle ride, touch football on the lawn, group dance à la *The Big Chill*, karaoke hour, bowling, sledding, or board games. Get outside to burn off some of the alcohol, calories, and old habits.

5. **DON'T ENCOURAGE UNDERAGE DRUNKS:** In her hilarious one-woman show, Elaine Stritch revealed her drinking problem started by tasting martinis she'd mixed for her parents as a teen in Detroit. Similarly, many alcoholics say their addiction began as kids, when they were offered booze at holiday bashes. Some teenagers

may have a genetic predisposition to alcoholism that you—and they—don't know of. Letting children sip from your beer mug or champagne flute sends a bad message that can backfire. Plus it's illegal. While creating a big taboo might impel teenagers to break it, asking for help serving food instead or having under-age guests share a holiday song, poem, or prayer with everyone is a much better way to make a child feel big and special.

6. **RETHINK RECIPES:** Although alcohol sometimes evaporates when you use it to cook, reconsider serving such old favorites as rum cakes, beer-boiled shrimp, and bourbon-mustard-glazed ham at guest-filled soirees over the holidays. Many people don't realize the dangerous dilemmas these ingredients can have for those batting the bottle. It's difficult to tell who has addiction issues. Alcohol-laced food might touch the lips of children, or trigger addiction issues from guests you're not aware are trying to stay sober. Even a tiny taste of alcohol can cause a relapse. When possible, try cooking "dry" this year. Added benefits: it's cheaper, healthier, and less fattening.

7. **BE AN EARLY BIRD:** It's easier to control the flow of liquor and its aftermath in daylight. Serve meals and host parties as early as possible, which parents with young children will appreciate. Mention it's "last call" while serving dessert. If there's a choice for postmeal parties, hold late-night rendezvous and gatherings at coffee houses, diners, and juice bars where Uncle Dave won't be as likely to overdo it in public or in front of minors.

8. **DRIVE IT HOME:** If you're serving liquor at your place, you should have alternative rides and routes available, whether it's a train schedule, phone for a car service, or designated driver. Yes, it's annoying when adults do not act responsibly for their own and their family's safe transportation, but imagine how you'll feel if your guest doesn't make it home or crashes his or her car on the highway. Now picture your child in the next lane.

9. **REDUCE STRESS:** Plane travel these days, followed by a big, out-of-town family reunion, does not equal serenity. More likely it

causes tension, conflicts, anxiety, and fights—huge triggers that could make anyone reach for a nightcap—or seven. So promote ways for yourself and everyone involved in your seasonal celebration to get enough sleep, exercise, eat well, and keep a normal routine. Acknowledge that some events, like meeting your in-laws for the first time, bringing babies or pets to a home where they've never been before, or introducing your new boyfriend or girlfriend to the family over Thanksgiving, could be emotionally fraught. In these cases, all-day affairs are not necessary. Think ahead and plan an excuse or escape route just in case. There's nothing wrong limiting the time frame of your visit. After three hours, if someone says "Oops, have to run to Aunt Lisa's for dessert," or "We're a bit under the weather," let them go without a scene, argument, or guilt trip.

Here are some presents that might help soothe savage, sloshed, or stressed out guests: prepaid cab fare or overnight hotel room, a gift certificate for a massage, manicure or pedicure, or a free pass to a local gym.

10. **DON'T BE EXTREME:** Thanksgiving, Hanukah, Christmas, Kwanzaa, and New Year's Eve are not the best time to push anybody to get sober cold turkey, quit drugs, start a strict diet, or put on the nicotine patch. Aim for moderation—and compassion—during the holidays. Then pick a specific quitting date in the near future.

CHAPTER 21

THE PROBLEM WITH DEPENDING ON PEOPLE

After thirty-eight years of estrangement, I desperately wanted to reconnect with my alcoholic mother before it was too late. Not to make amends, really. I just wanted to see her once and not be afraid. Over the last five years I courted her, sending flowers, fruit, and candy for her birthday and holidays, asking to visit. She acknowledged my gifts with terse handwritten notes. She sent back the designer jelly beans with the scrawl: "I prefer dark chocolate." She used to ignore me completely or end with "you stupid idiot." So we were making progress.

At a conference in Colorado three summers ago, I bought her a wooden souvenir that said "A box for all your dreams" with her name, Mary, engraved on the side. She wrote back, "I'll put my dreams in it. My arthritis is so bad I have no feeling in my fingers. I can't even drive. I dream the feeling will come back." I dreamt her maternal feelings for me would surface before she died. Yet she still refused to see me.

This horrible rift had been going on since I was nineteen and made harsh, yet true, statements about the horrors of living with her alcoholism at the custody trial for my younger sister. I had broken my family's unstated code that nobody was ever allowed to reveal my mother's drinking problem. She was obviously still enraged that I'd publicly flaunted her rules of secrecy. When my sister, who was ten, moved in with my father, my mother had cut off all contact with me and never looked back.

Now, as a fifty-nine-year-old psychologist, I was finally starting to link my substance abuse specialty to growing up with a violent, abusive drunk. Although I constantly told all of my patients "Addicts depend on substances, not people," and advised them throughout recovery to "Lead the least secretive life you can," I admit that I wound up regretting that I had spoken out publicly against my mother. No child should ever have to testify against a parent.

Last winter I received a longer, charming thank-you note from her signed "With Love," which was very uncharacteristic. It turned out a speech therapist had written it for her. I soon received a call from a doctor friend of the family warning that, at eighty-nine, my mother was frail and fading fast. She resided in a high-end nursing home in Dallas. She showed signs of dementia after a stroke and couldn't hear or walk well. If she couldn't write or speak, she could no longer refuse me.

After almost forty years apart, I made the six-hour drive with my wife and twelve-year-old daughter, Kathy. Although my mother was speechless, in our hour and a half together she responded to my statements and queries with body movements, nods, and scowls that showed she clearly knew me. Not that she was happy to see me or nice. She was herself: determined, prideful, mean. When I handed her a bar of dark chocolate, her shaking hand slowly pulled it to the edge of the table and let it drop to the floor, then she stepped on it. Twice. Did she fear I might poison her?

"I know this is hard for you. I get it," I said calmly, picking it up and putting it in front of her again. "But I'm not going to hurt you. You don't have to take my candy if you don't want to." Then she ate it.

Mary smiled at my wife, who was strong, smart, and willful, traits my mother respected. She stared at my daughter so intently it spooked Kathy. I guessed Kathy looked like Mary had seventy-seven years earlier. When we went to leave, I asked my mother if I could hug her. She nodded and I did. But then she drew back and wouldn't budge. She wanted to leave but would not pass by with me standing so close to her. Kathy whispered, "She needs you to move further away from her first, Dad." After I did, Mary shuffled by.

My mother had also cut off my siblings over the years, so out of the four of us I was the only one to see her sick. My brothers and sister were shocked since Mary always hated me the worst, even before I'd spoken out at my parents' divorce trial. Was it because I looked the most like her? I was the smallest, weak and sick as an infant. She once screamed that she had wanted to let me die, like an injured animal. Did I forgive her? Absolutely not. Would I protect her now if she needed anything? Yes. On the ride home, my daughter said what my mother could not: "You are a good son."

As we drove home, I thought, "I am stronger than my mother now. She's a fragile old woman who can no longer physically hurt me." If I wanted to, I could overpower her. But I didn't want to anymore.

A month later I returned to visit her with a photograph of Mary as a young, beautiful actress. It was taken of her cameo in a 1946 movie called *Bedlam* with Boris Karloff. Ironically she had played a deaf mute. Now she appeared fascinated by her old image, pleased when I showed the staff who she used to be. They knew I was coming in advance this time so they had spruced her up. Her cheeks looked pinker, her gray hair puffy. I couldn't help my childlike thoughts, "She's not dying. She will live forever."

We were both more comfortable this time. She never pulled away, frowned, or shook her head no. I felt relieved and lighter. Then I wondered if she just liked the attention. When I pointed to a cell phone picture of Kathy, whom she had met the last trip, she had no idea who Kathy was. Perhaps my mother was only acting warm to me because she had lost her mind.

Before I left, I asked about the nursing home's alcohol policy. They allowed her to have one glass of wine at 3:30 PM, which she did every single day. That she never forgot.

ACKNOWLEDGMENTS

I would like to express my heartfelt thanks to:

My literary agent Ryan Harbage, Skyhorse Publishing editors Jay Cassell, Ann Treistman, and Yvette Grant, publisher Tony Lyons, publicists Jennifer Doerr, Lauren Cutler, and Barb Burg, magazine editors Carla Flora, John Glassie, Carrie Sloan & Amy Klein for their endless support and immeasurable help in making *Unhooked* a reality.

For their critical brilliance on early drafts: Rebecca Wiegand, Stephen Gaydos, Devan Sipher, Jami Bernard, Alice Feiring, Kimberlee Auerbach, Kate Walter, Hilary Davidson, Royal Young, Rich Prior, Tony Powell, Ami Angelowicz, Lisa Lewis, Jeff Nishball, Sara Karl, Judy Batalion, Aly Gerber, Tasha Gordon & David Brand.

To my most important mentors: the late Christine Duffey, Richard M. Billow, Robert Mendelsohn & my father-in-law E. G. Bradberry.

For their devotion to the difficult work at the Village Institute and the difficult work of working with me: my colleagues Claudia Andrei, Robert Bradberry, Carrie Nickles, Yas Soans, Joye Henrie, Chelsey Miller, Lynn Horridge, Josh Jonas, Enid Zuckerman, Cassie Kaufmann, Petra Amrani, Emily Ogden, Patrick McNulty, Ruth Zeligman, Alessandra Sternberg & Michael Ritter.

Mostly I would like to thank my two sons, my daughter, and my wife for their infinite patience and for showing me by example that the worst possible circumstances can be turned into life's greatest triumphs.

ABOUT THE AUTHORS

FREDERICK WOOLVERTON, PHD, is a clinical psychologist who has specialized in treating addiction patients for more than twenty-five years. He earned his doctoral degree from Adelphi University, was the clinical director of the Baldwin Council Against Drug Abuse in Long Island, and is the founder of The Village Institute For Psychotherapy in Manhattan and Arkansas, which provides a range of psychological services including teaching and treatment of addictive disorders. He has given workshops and conferences at the New York State Psychological Association, the Derner Institute of Advanced Psychological Studies, Pace University, the Northwest Arkansas Psychology Association, as well as working with the police, firemen, and Red Cross helping parents who lost children on 9/11 at the World Trade Center. His work has appeared in *The New York Times*, *Psychology Today*, and AOL. His website is www.villageinstitute.com.

SUSAN SHAPIRO is the author of seven previous books including *Lighting Up* and *Speed Shrinking*, both based on her own successful addiction therapy with Dr. Woolverton. For twenty years she has been an award-winning journalism professor at The New School and New York University, where she currently teaches her popular "Instant Gratification Takes Too Long" classes and seminars. Her work has appeared in *The New York Times*, *Washington Post*, *Boston Globe*, *Los Angeles Times*, *Newsweek*, *Nation*, *People*, *More*, *Glamour*, *Marie Claire*, *Salon.com* and *Daily Beast*. She has appeared on *The Today Show*, *Weekend Today*, *The Morning Show*, CNN, NY1, E! Entertainment, LX-TV, and the BBC. Her website is www.susanshapiro.net.